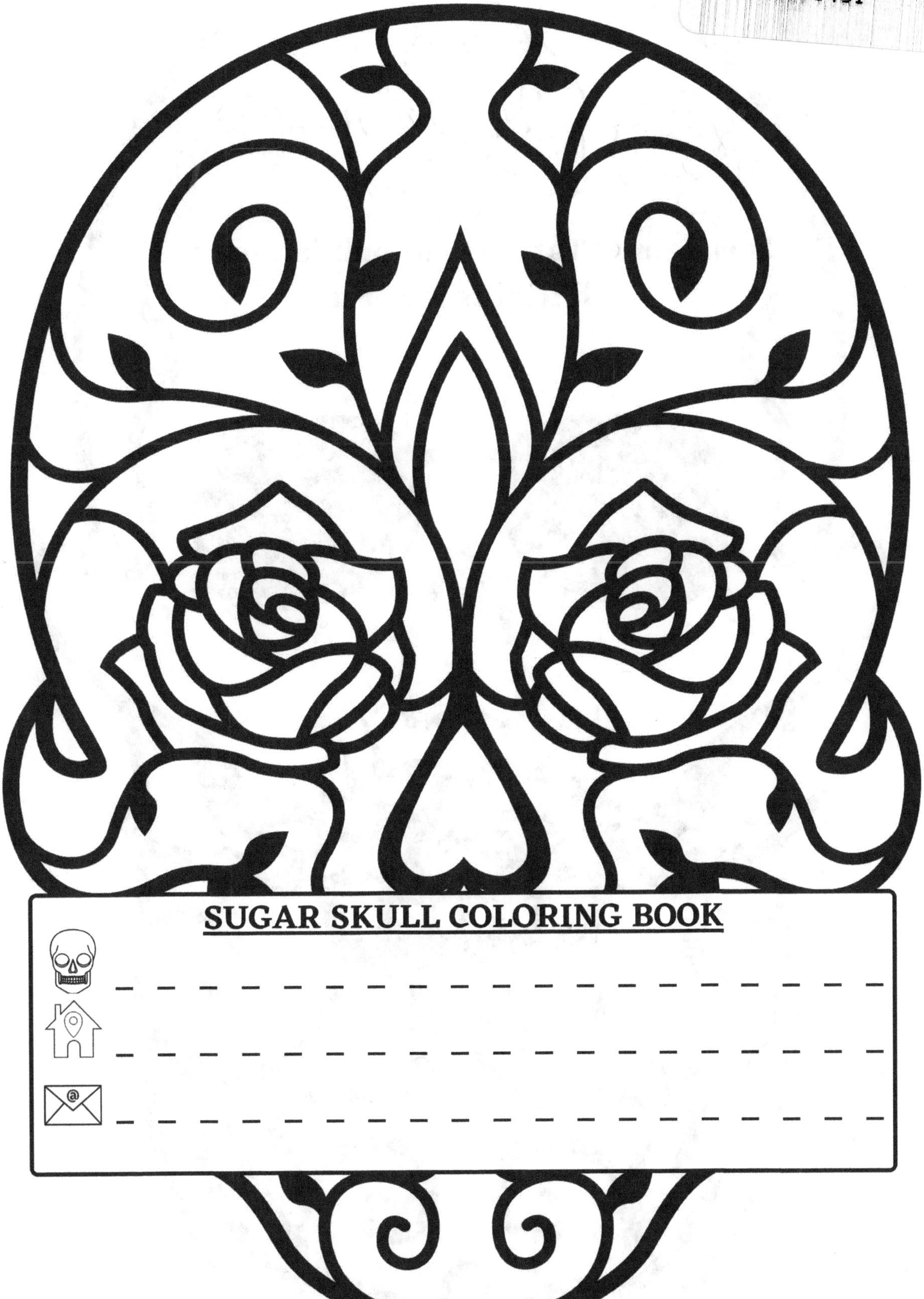

SUGAR SKULL COLORING BOOK

Copyright © Tattoo twin publishing 2020
All Rights Reserved

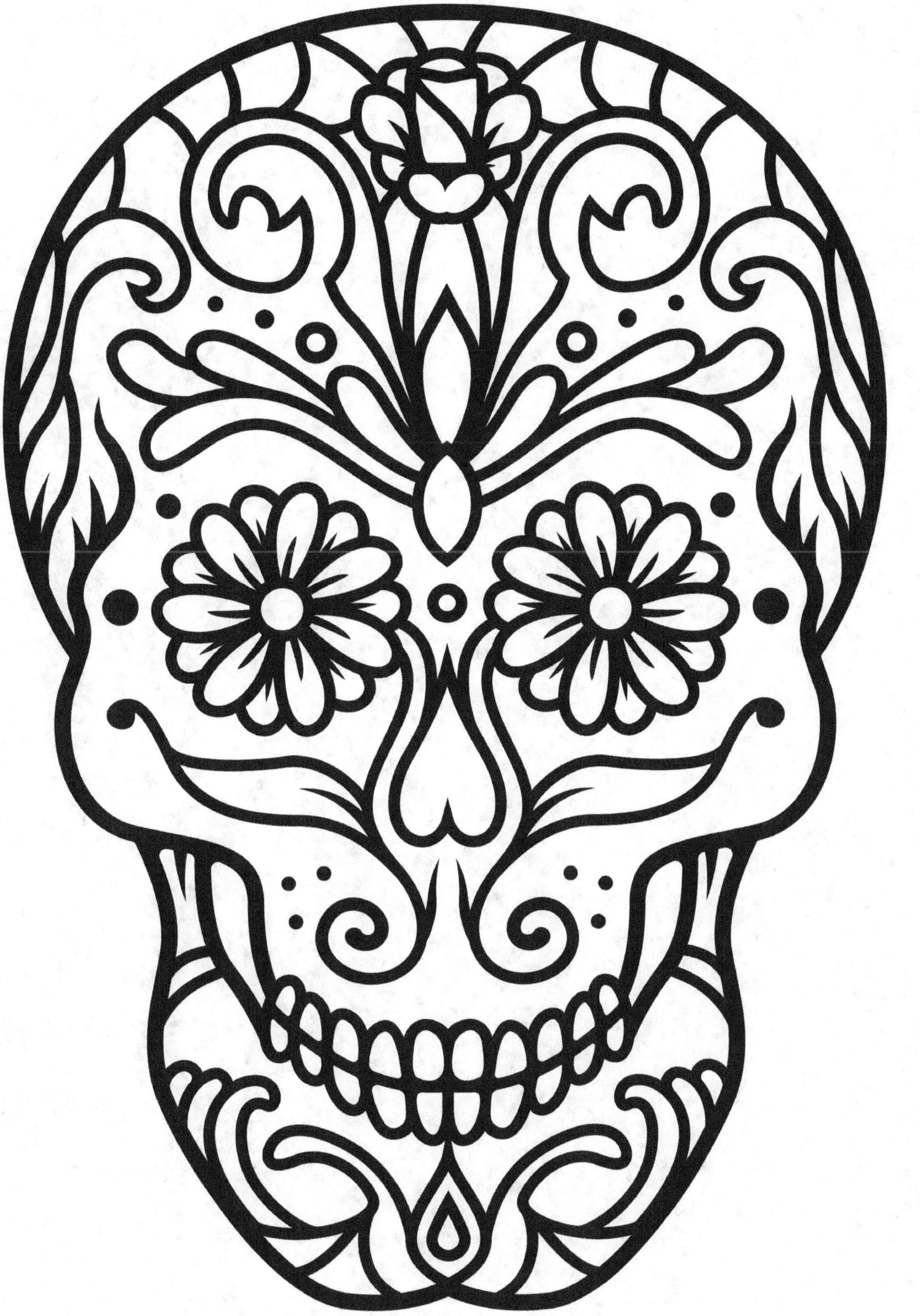

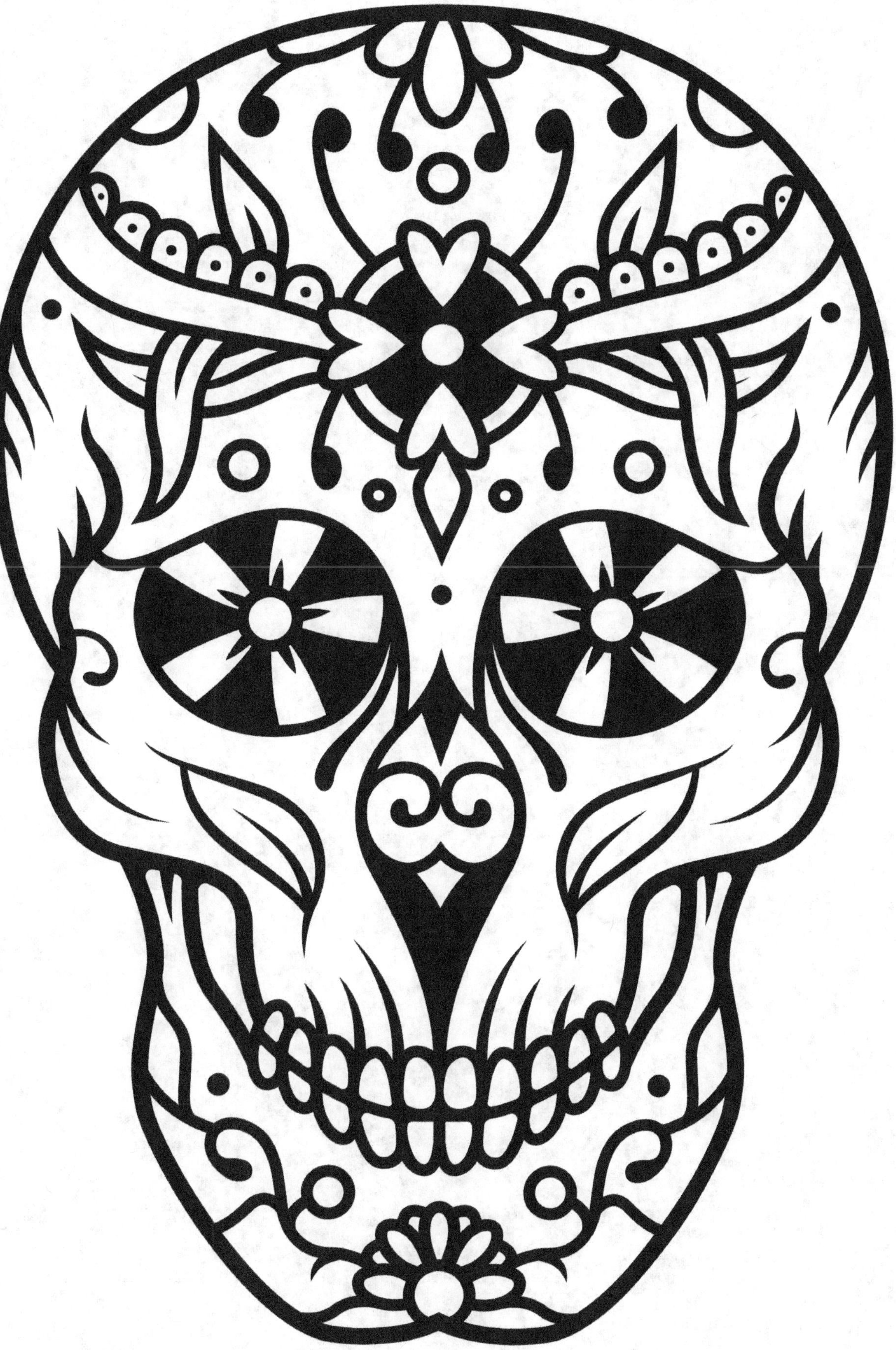

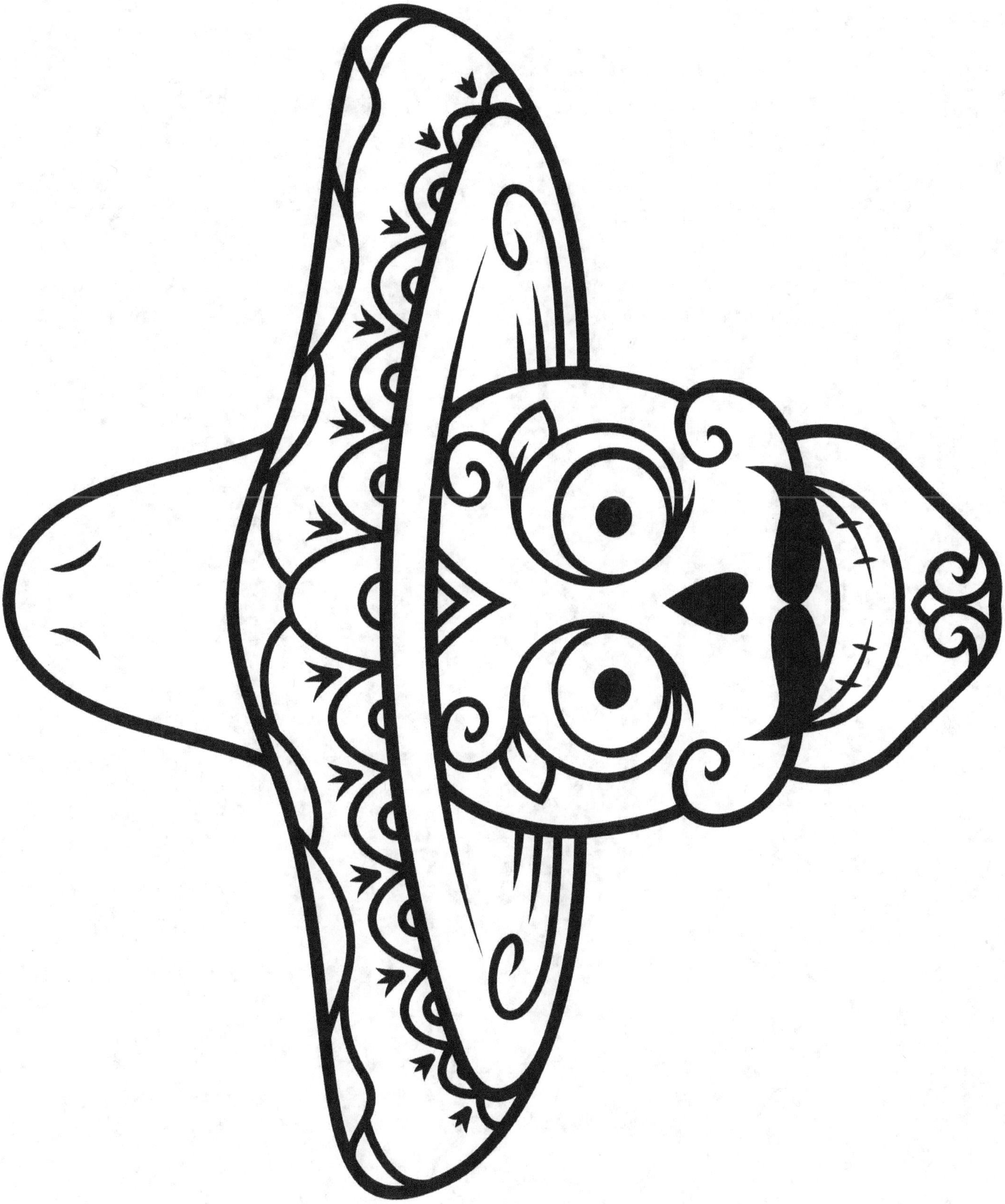

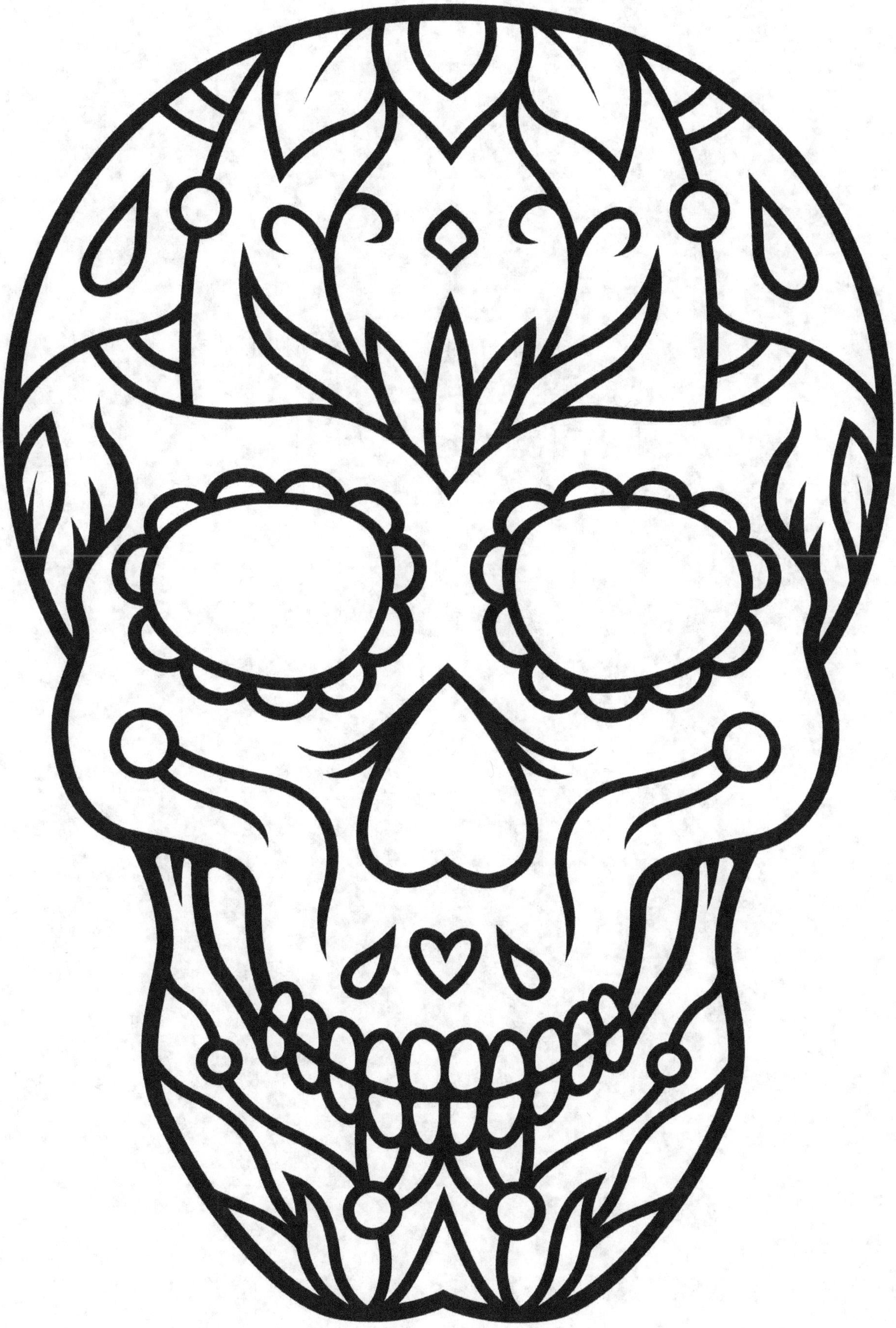

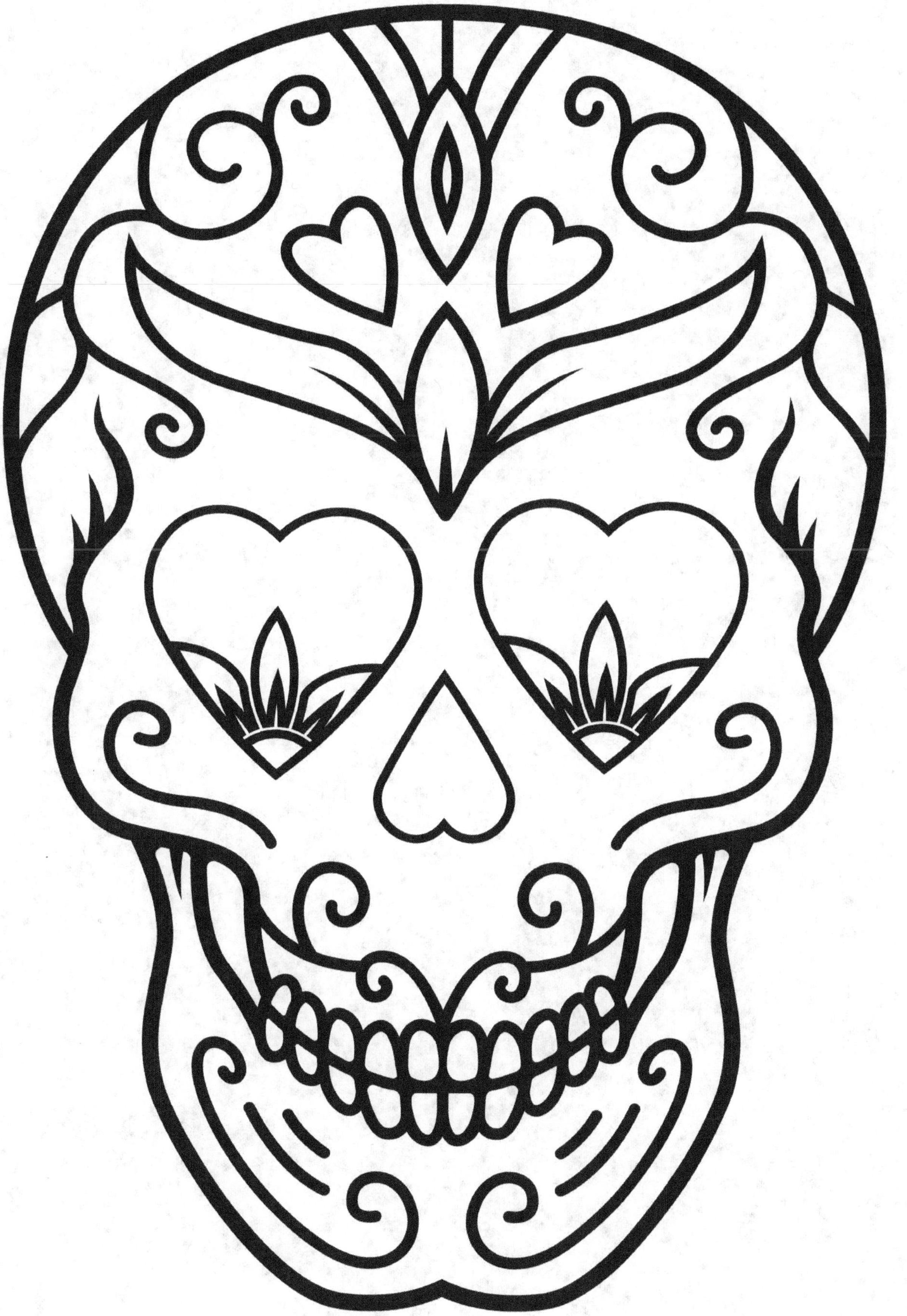

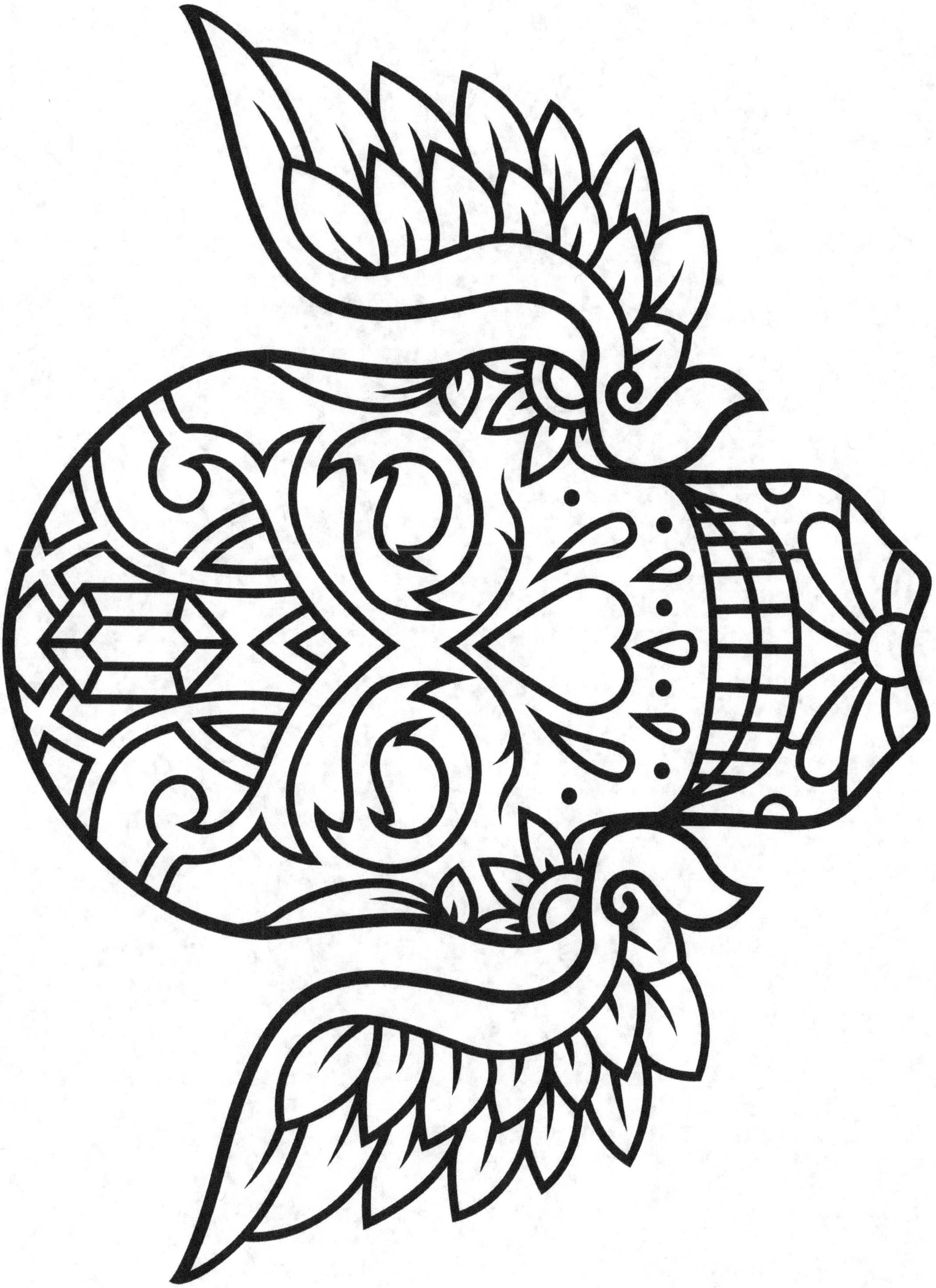

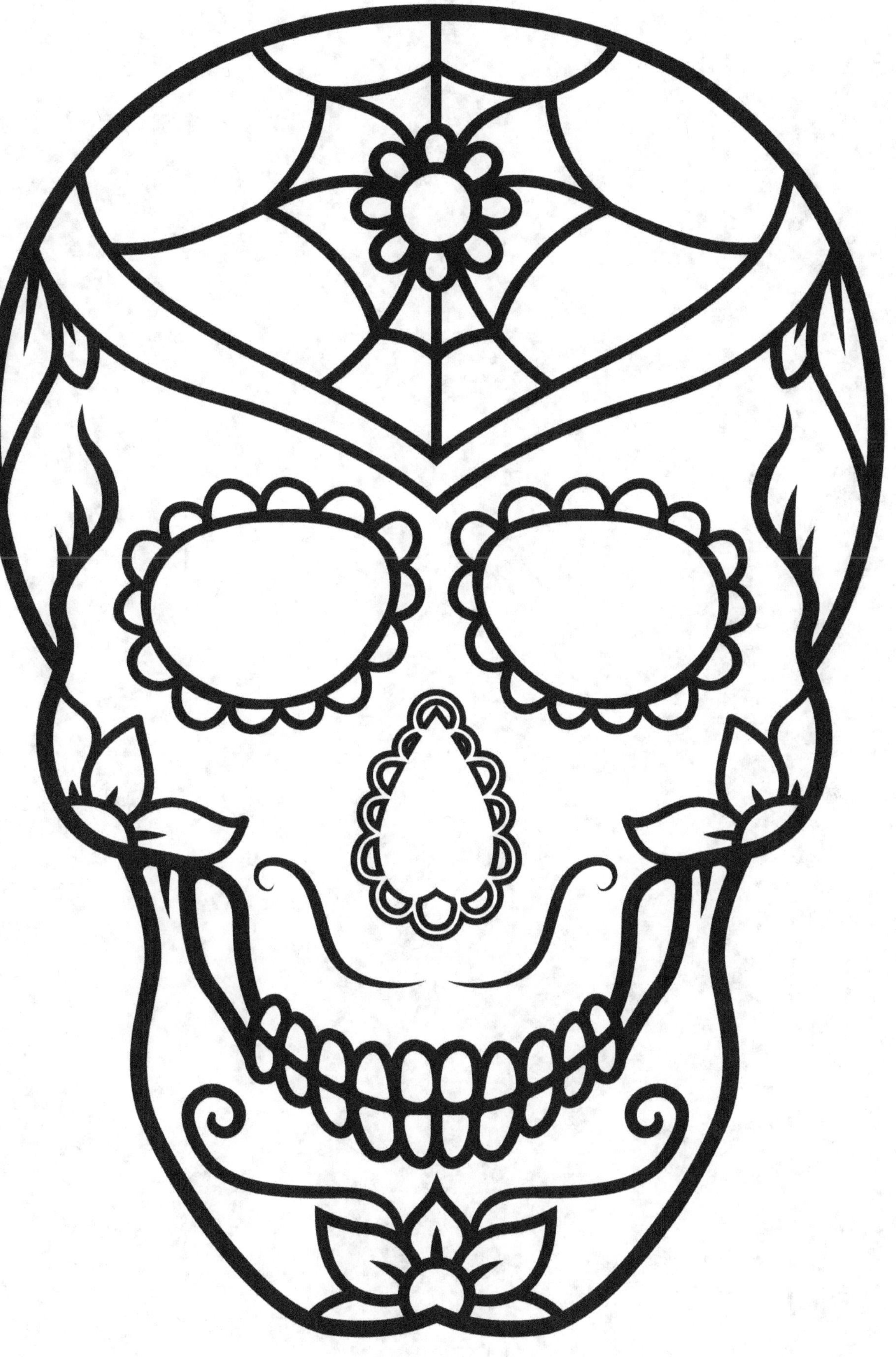

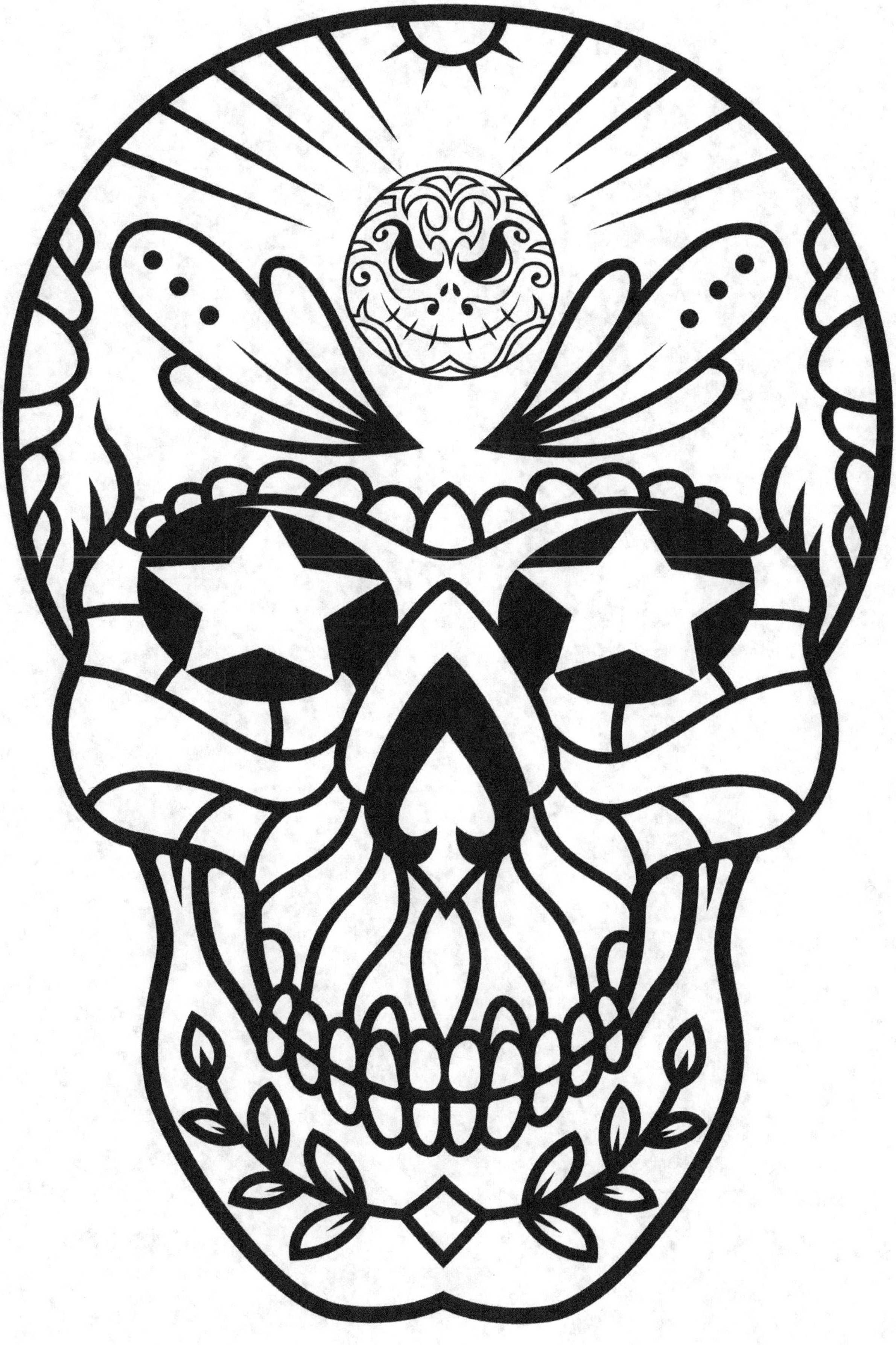

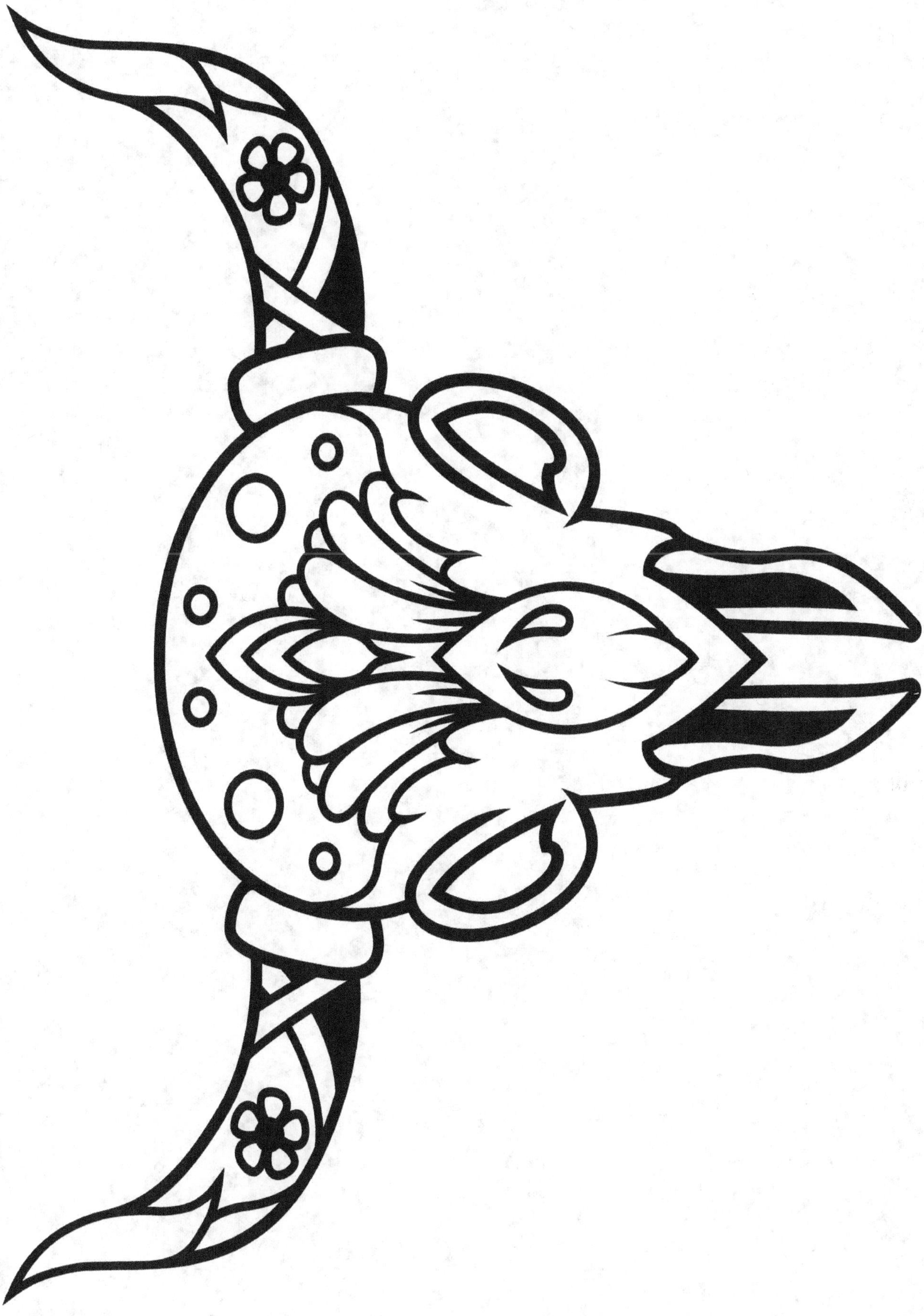

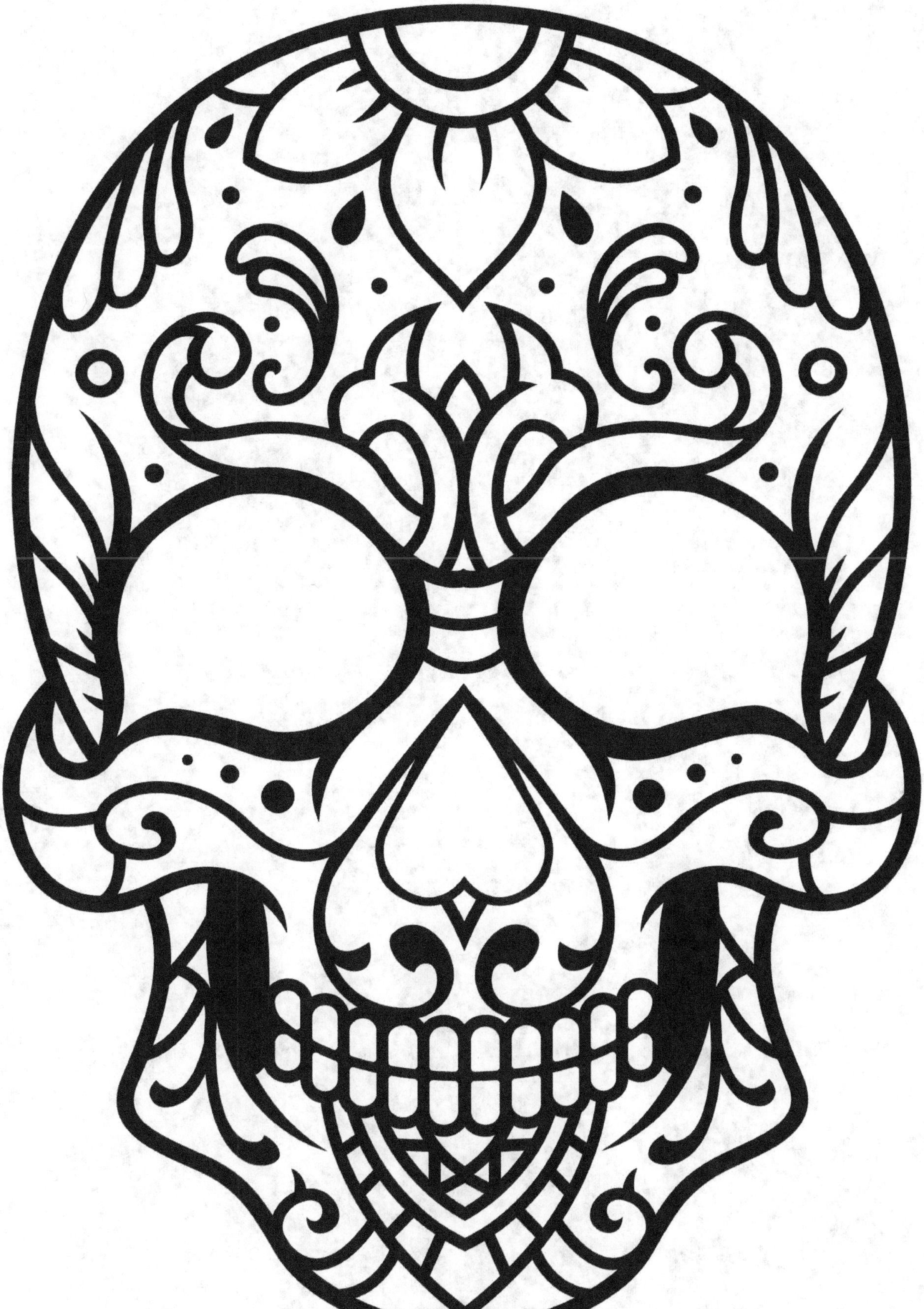

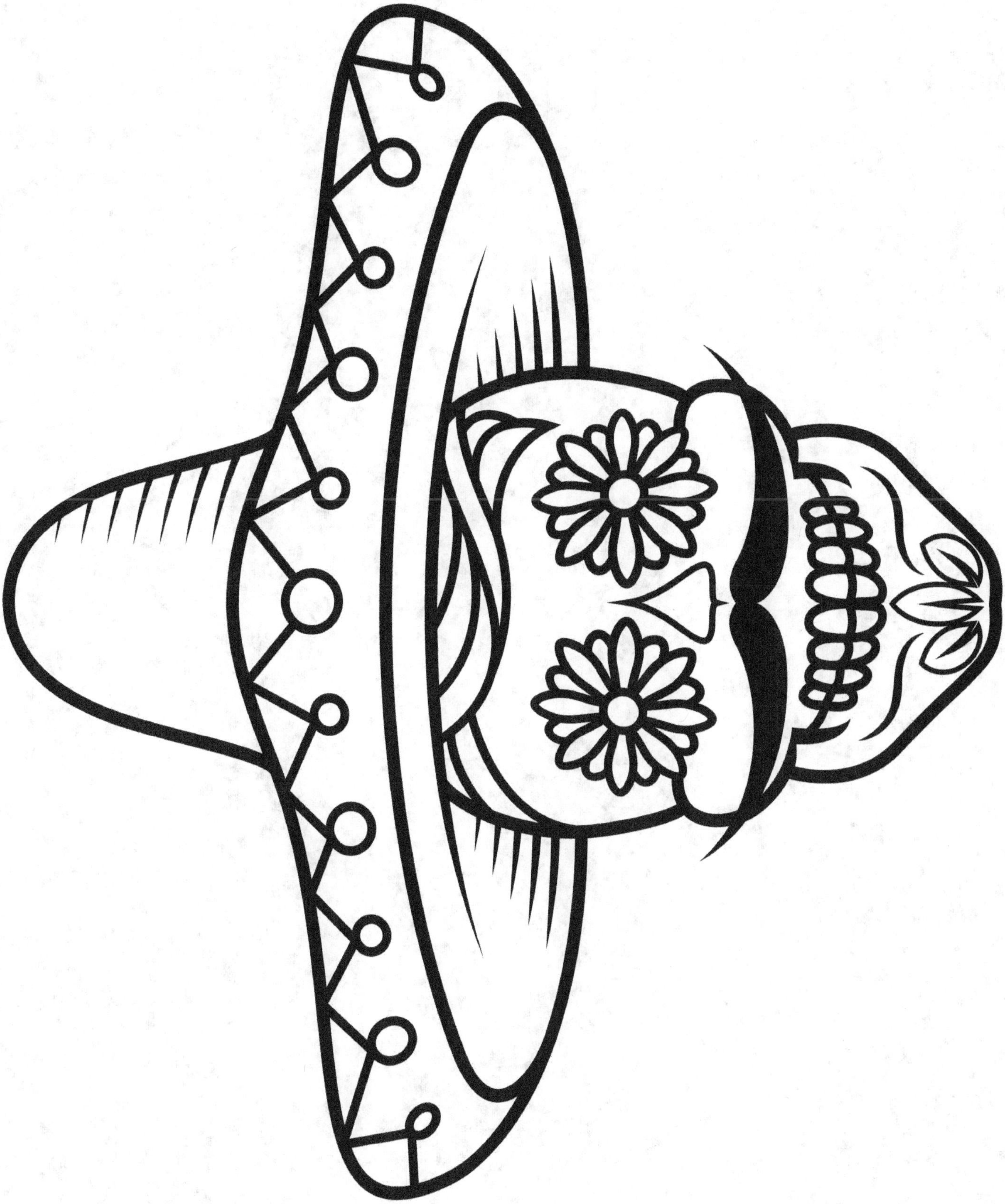

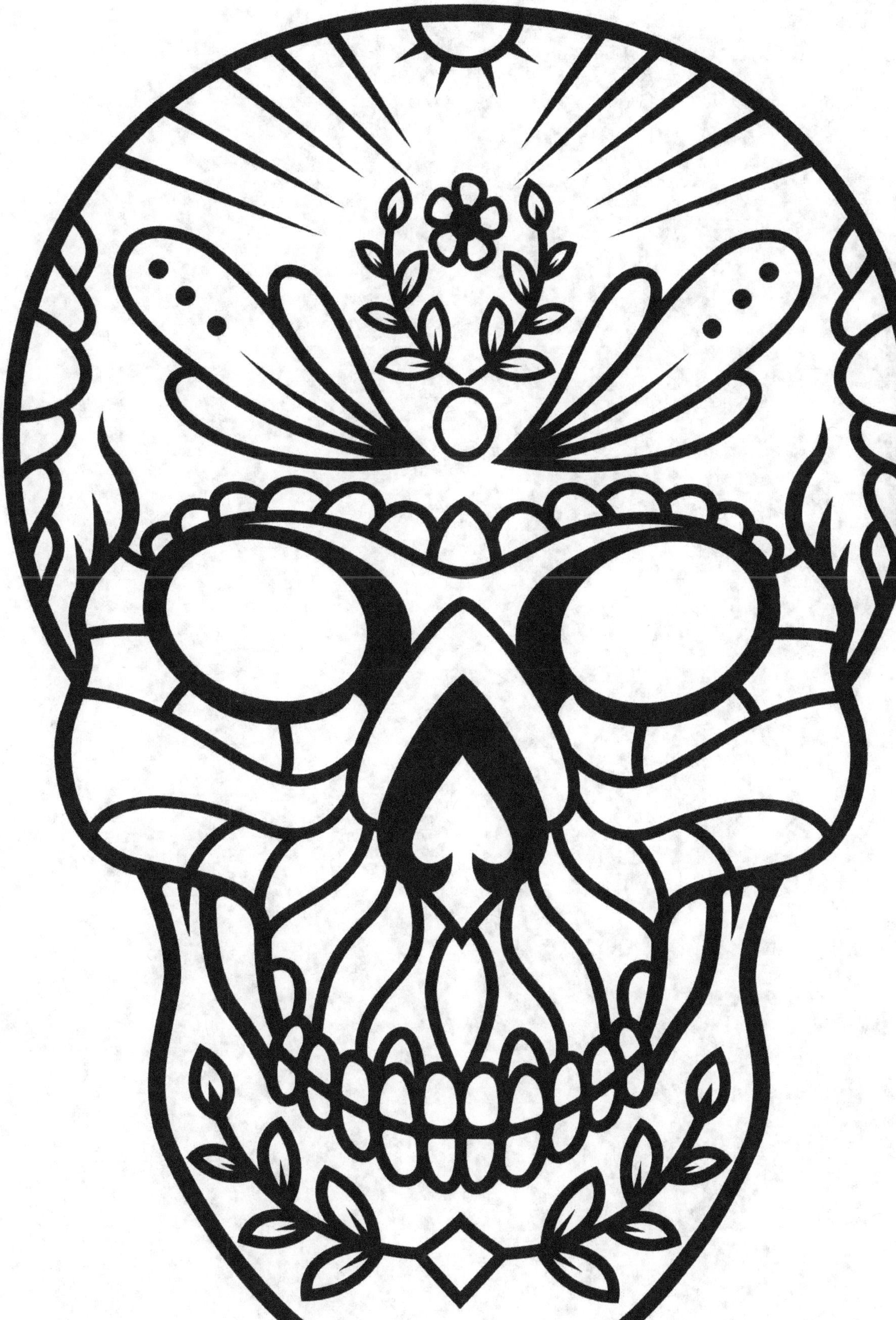

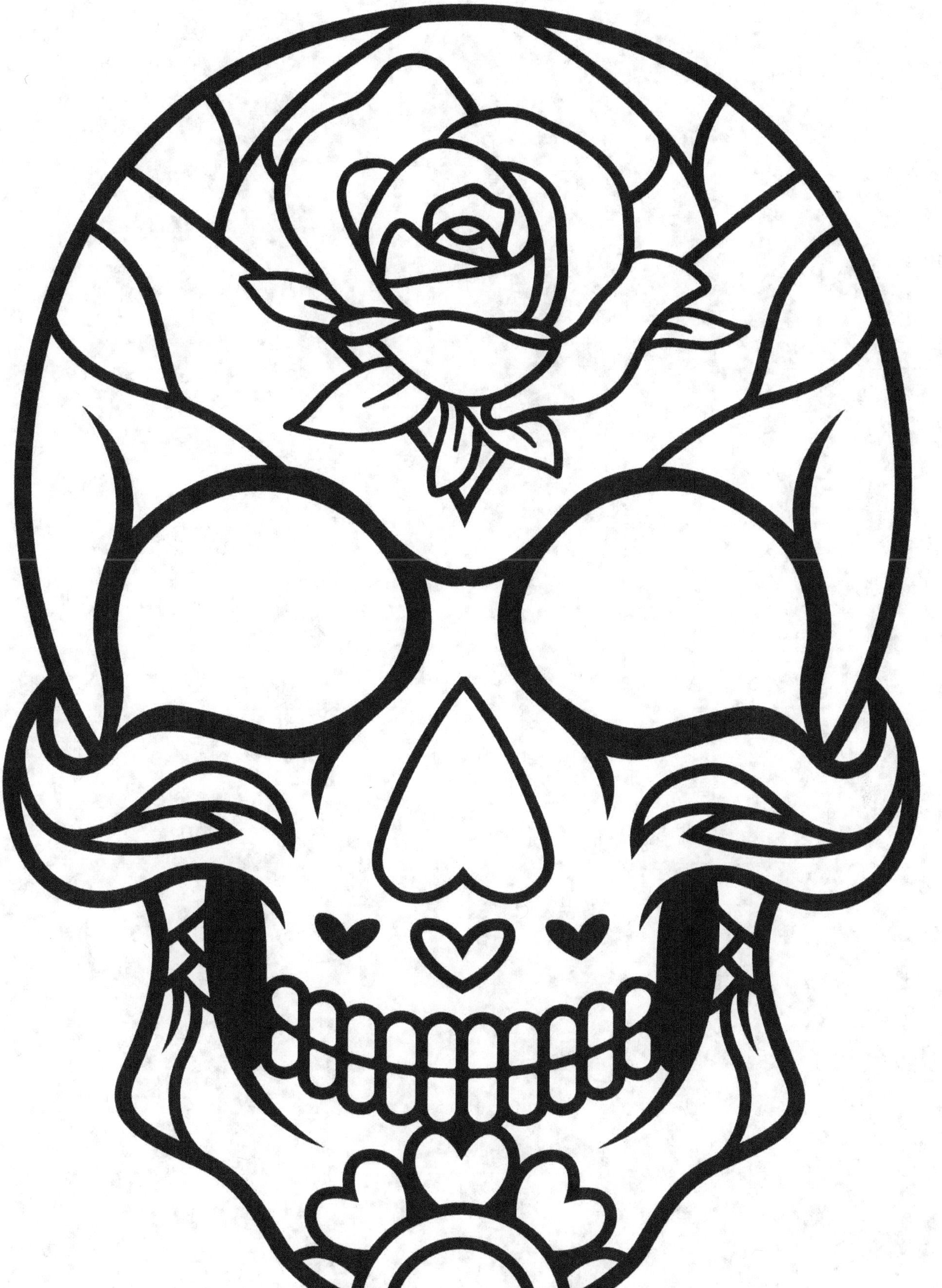

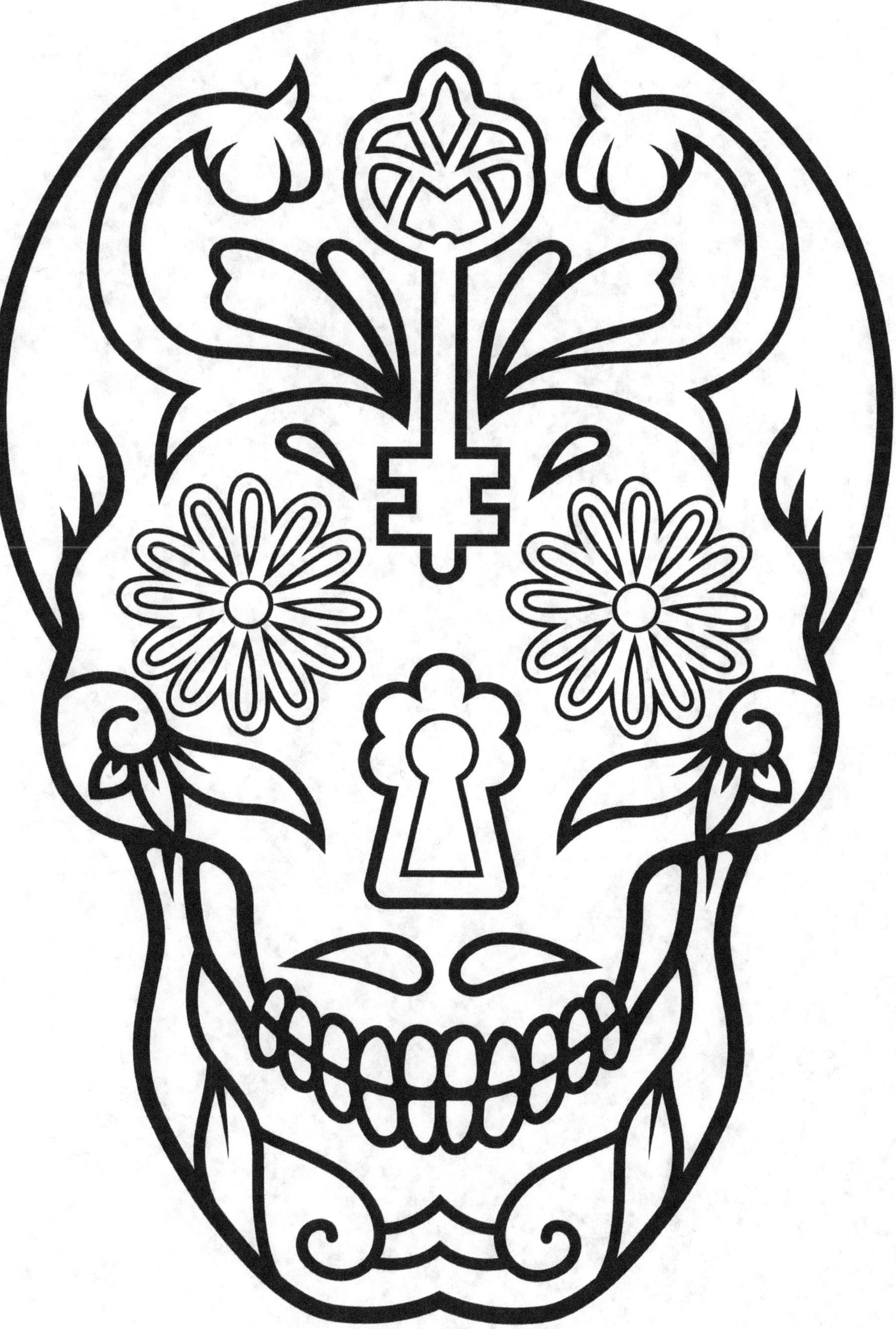

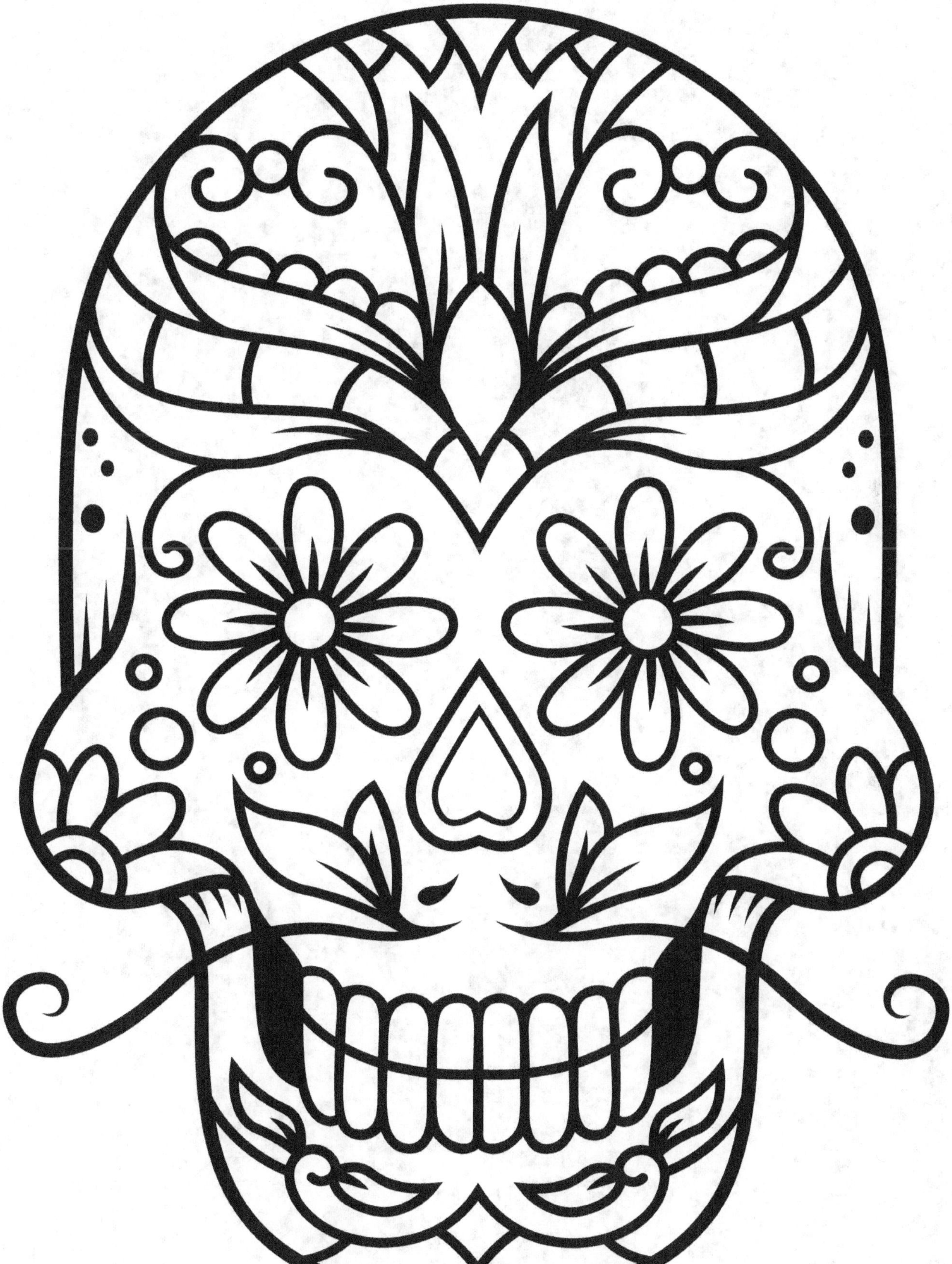

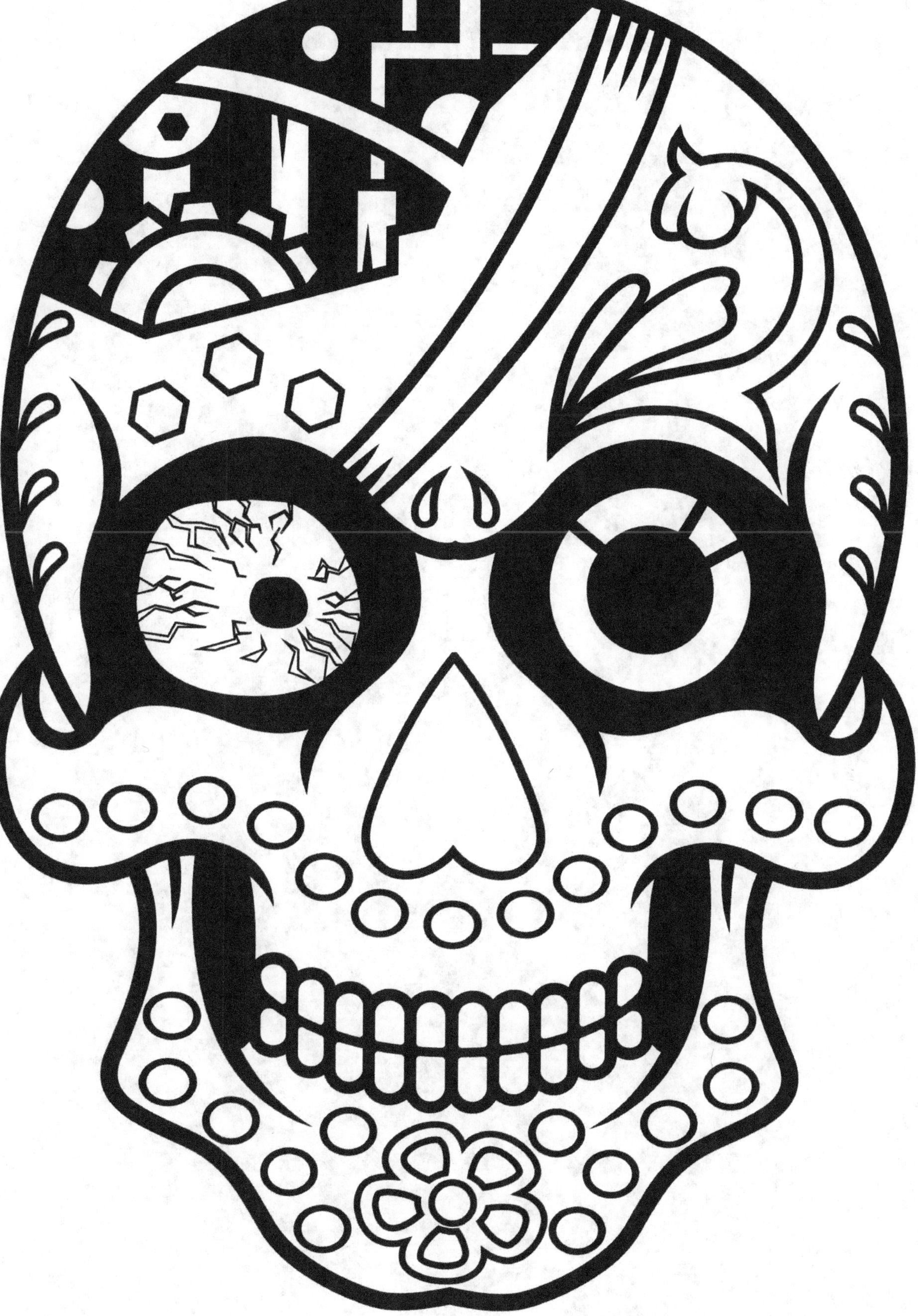

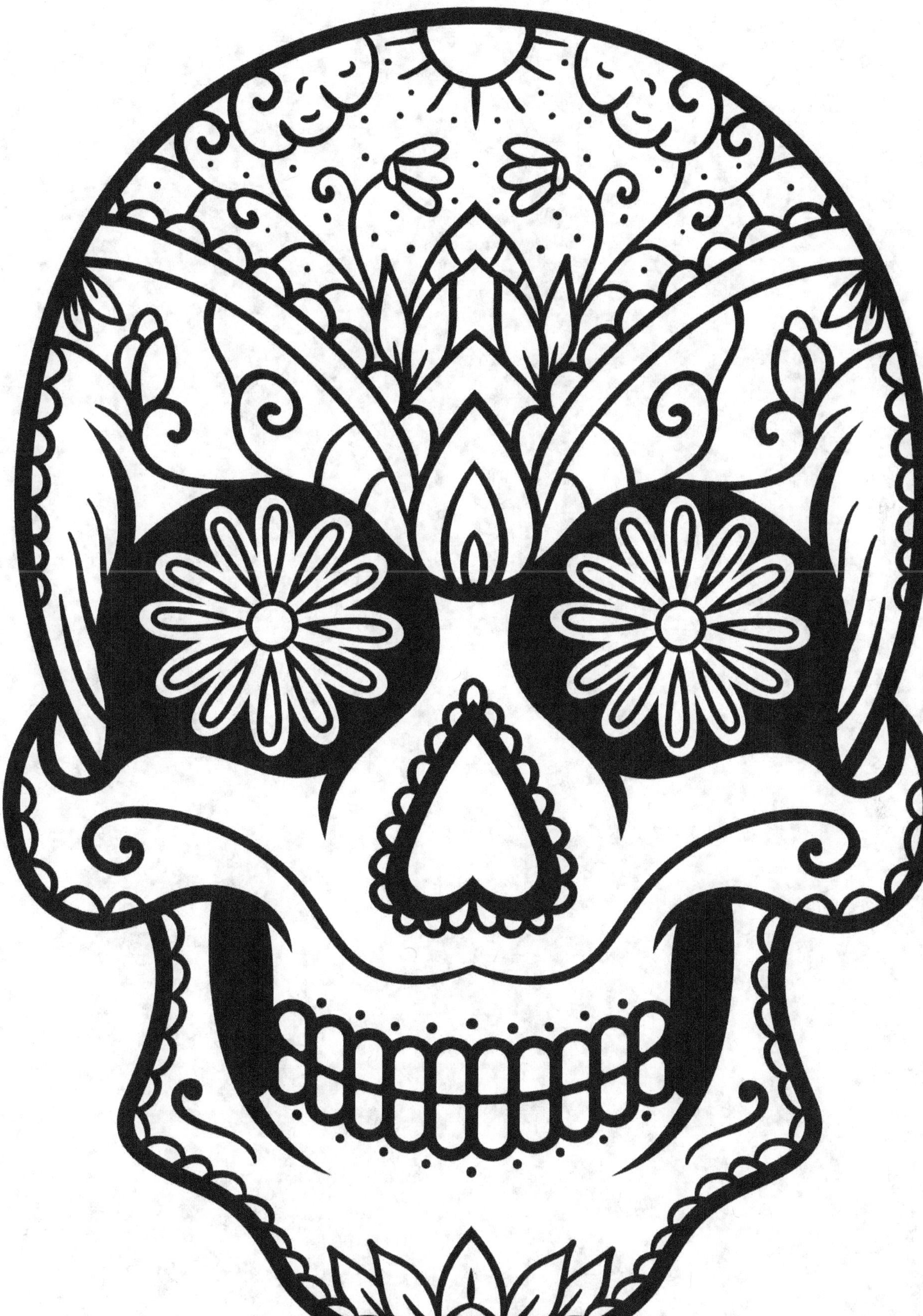

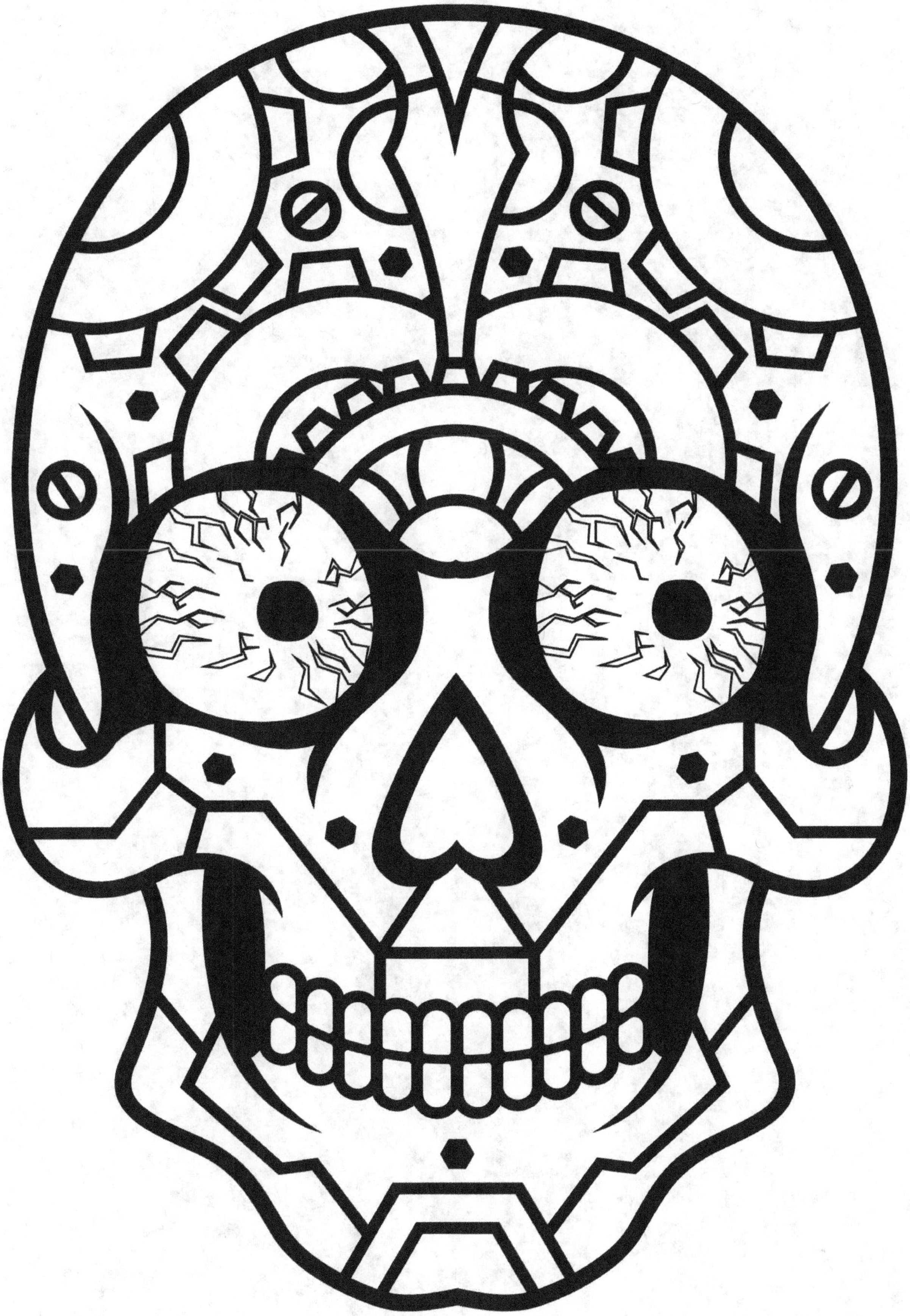

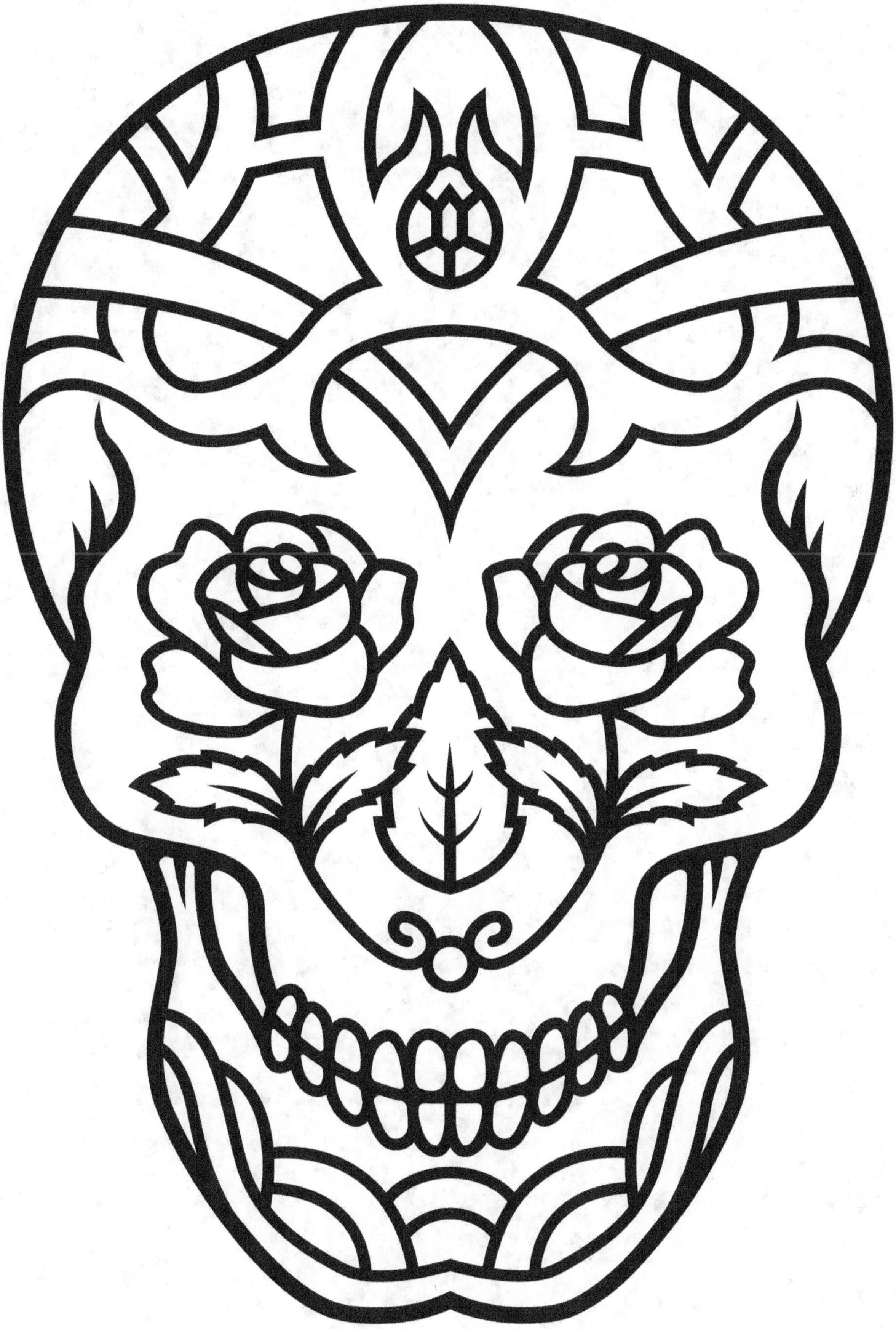

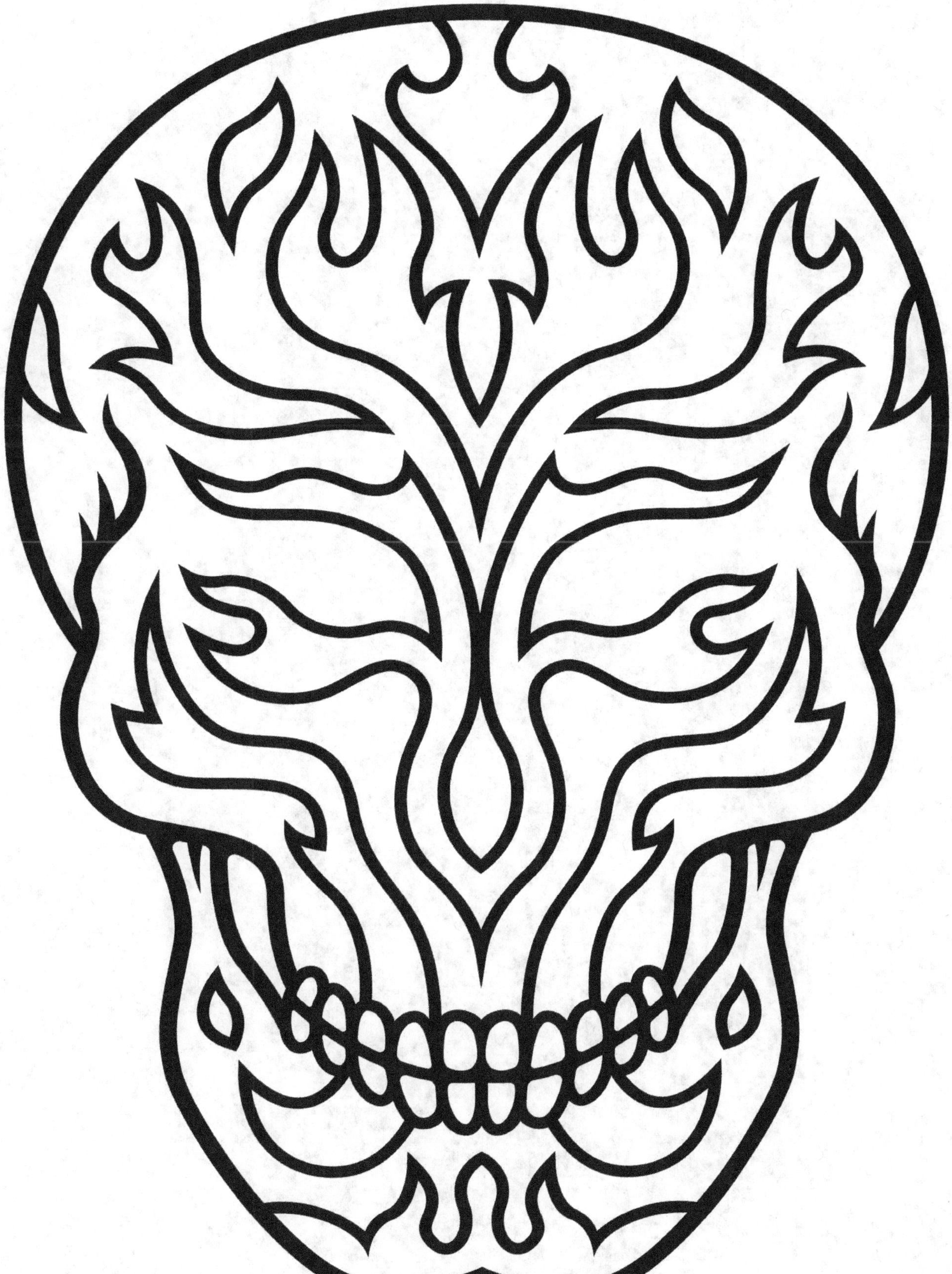

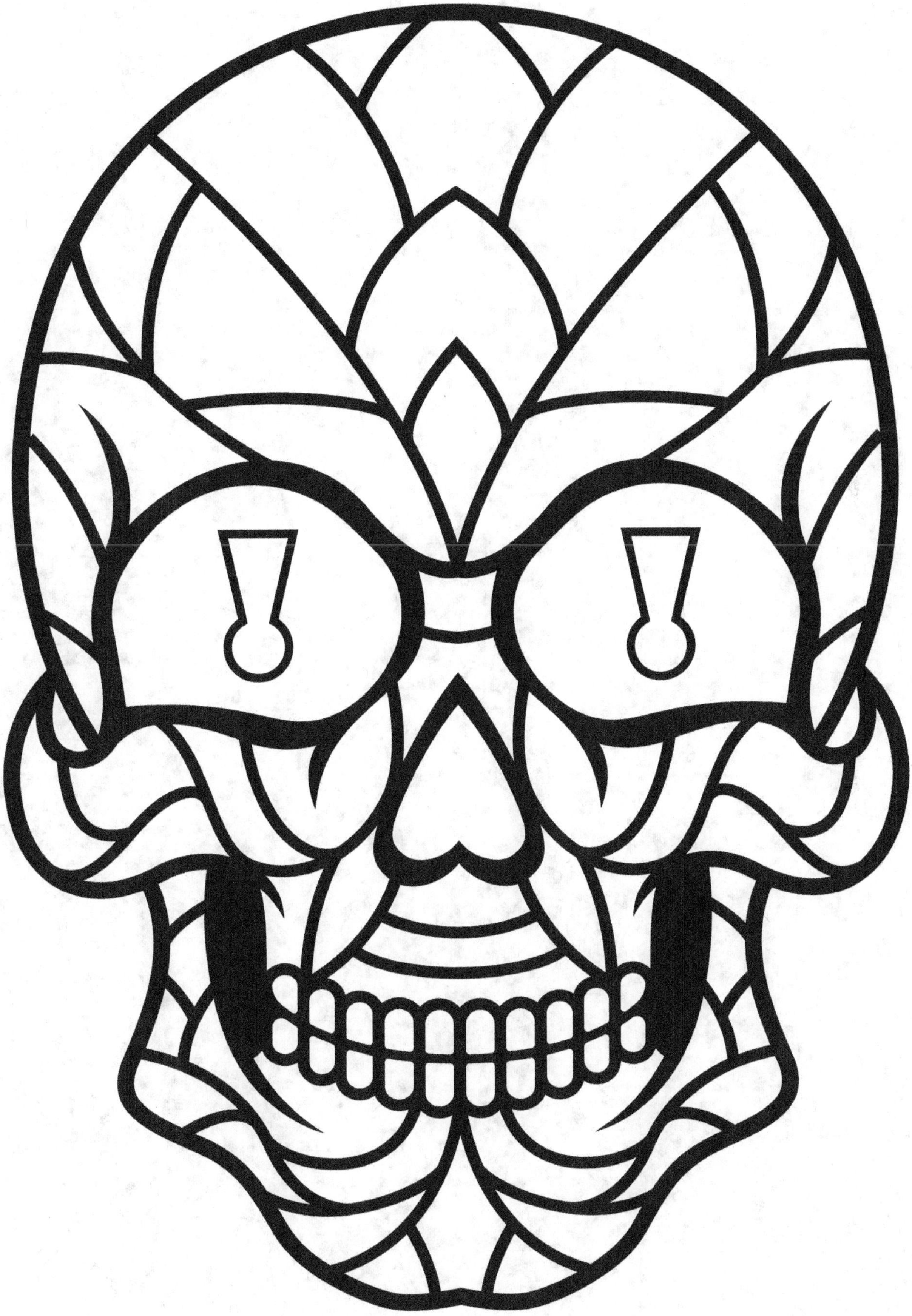

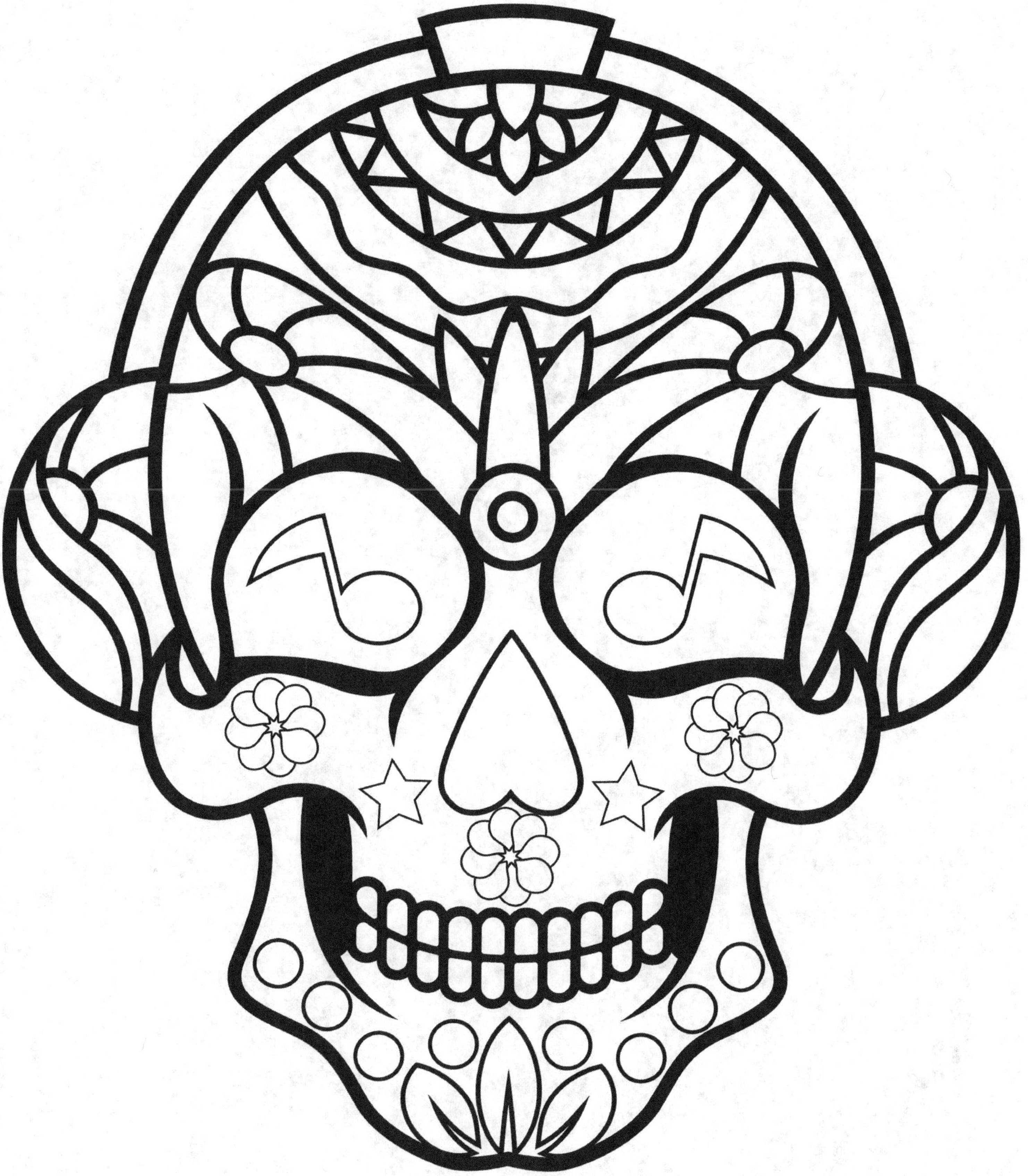

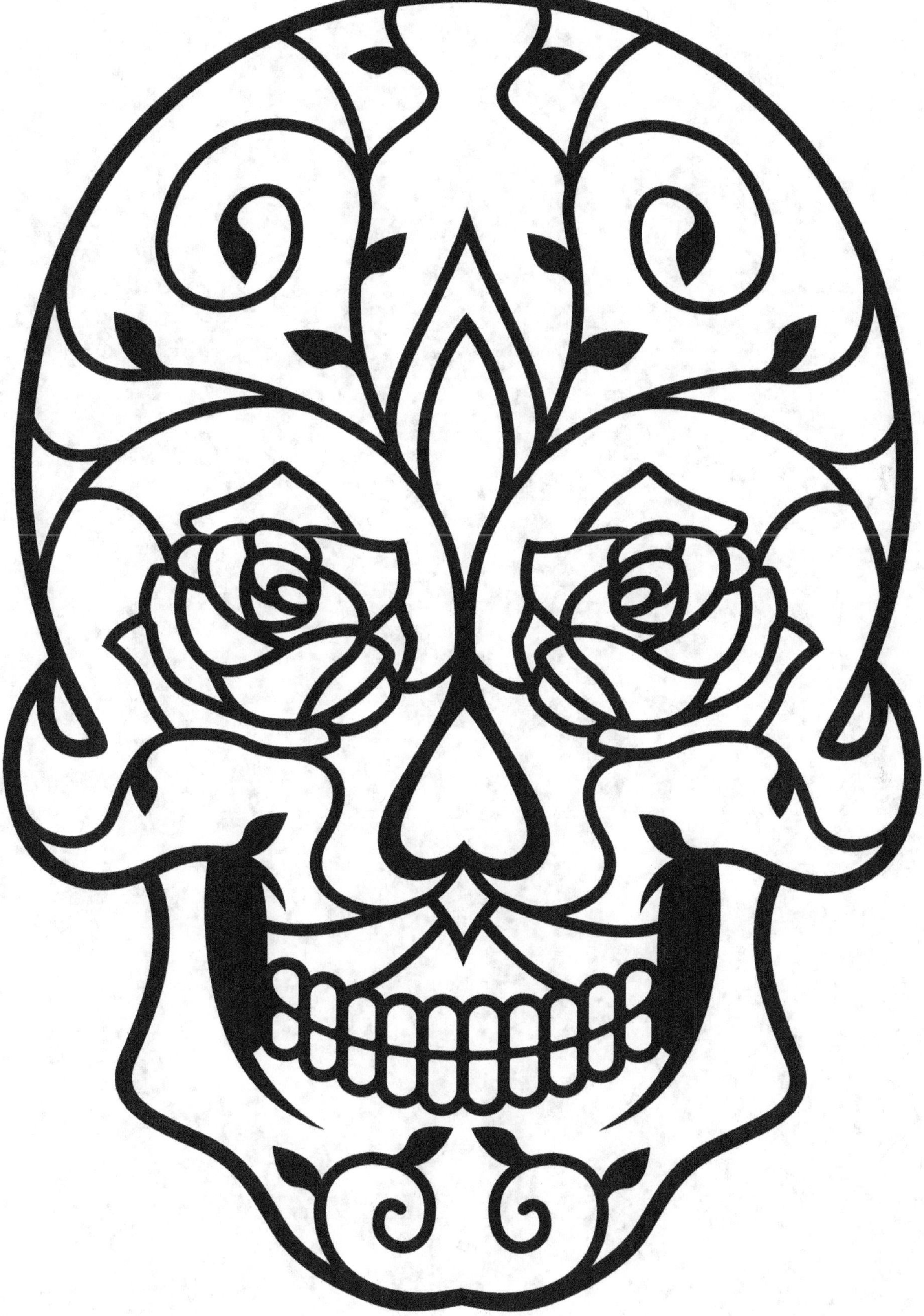

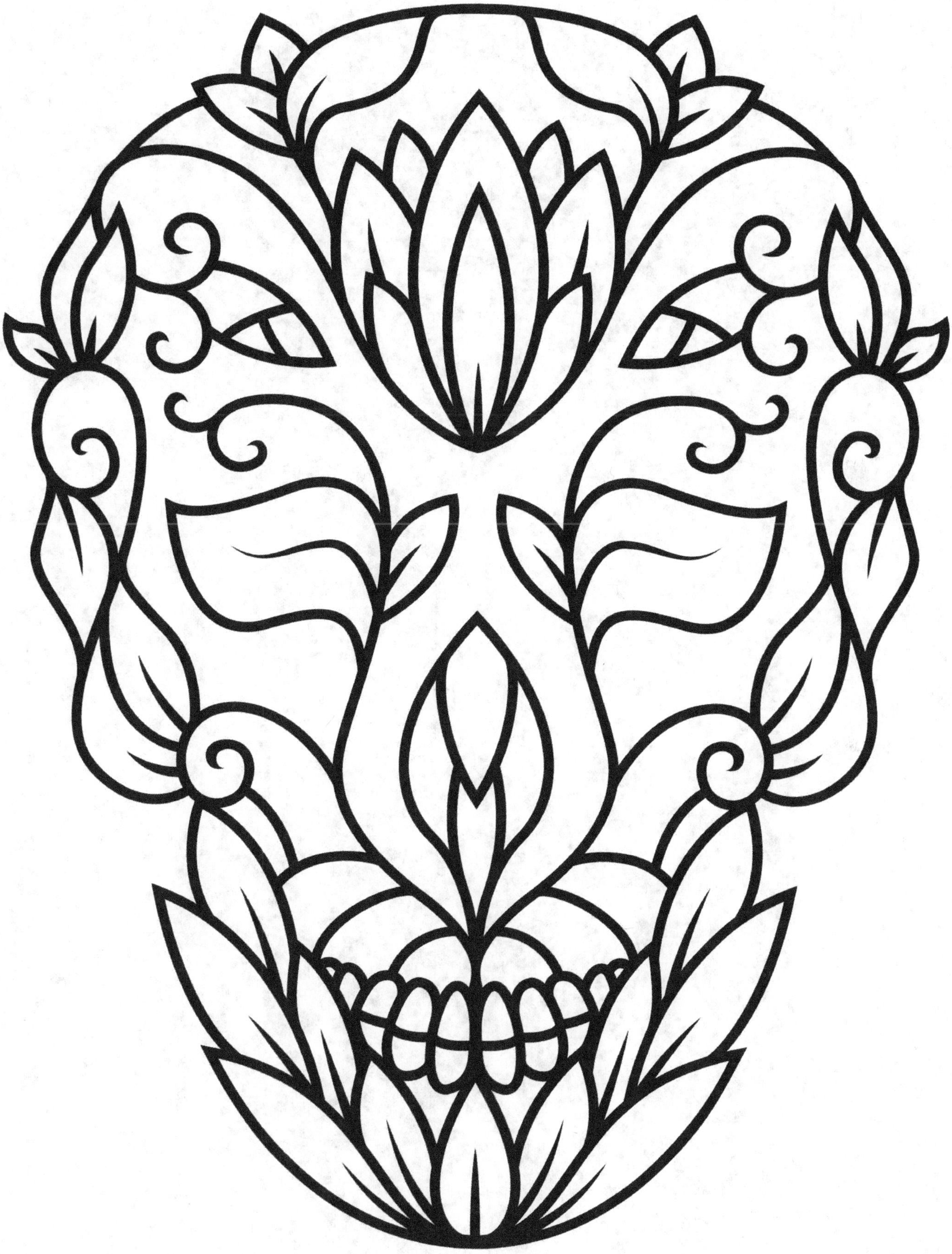

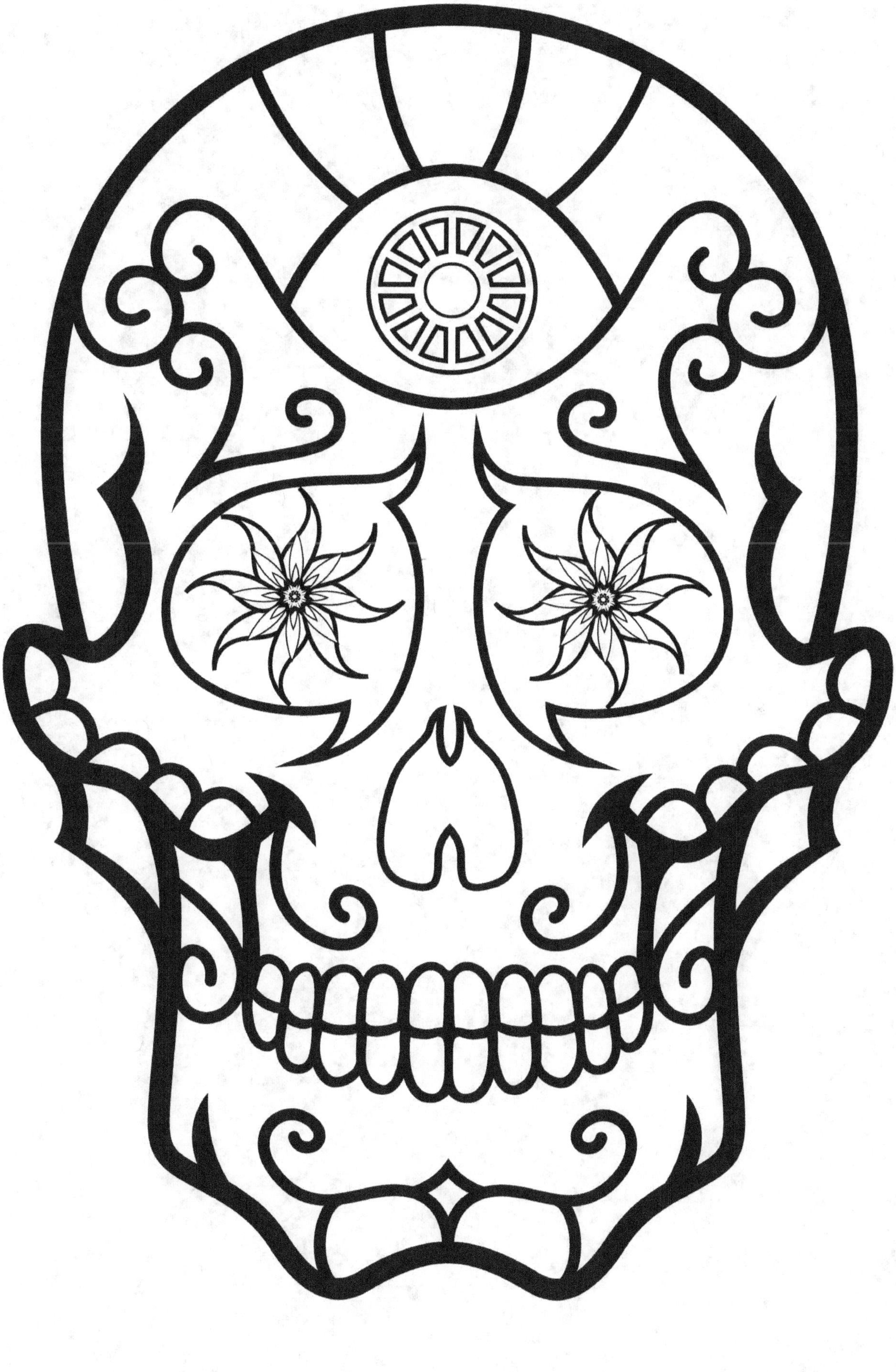

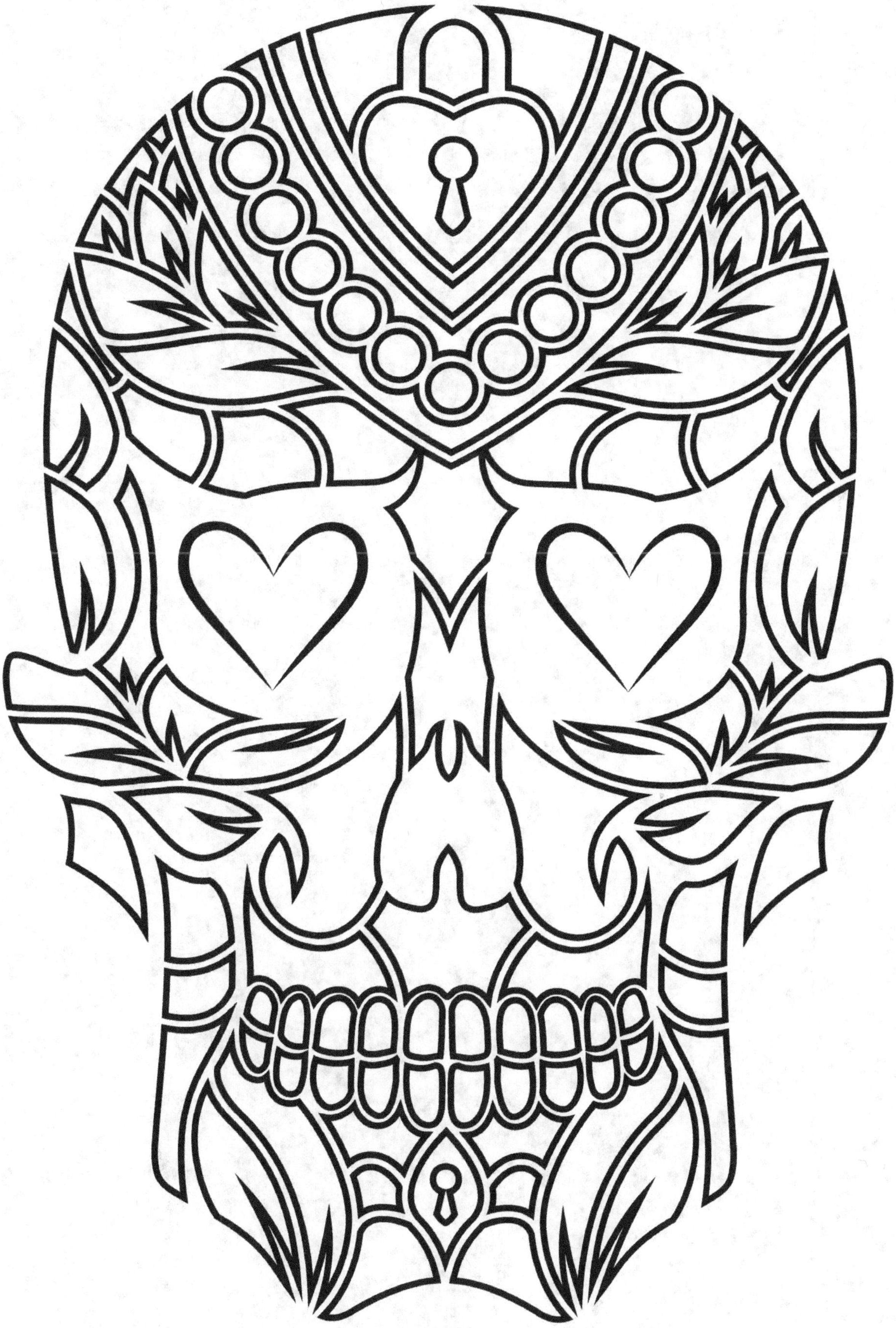

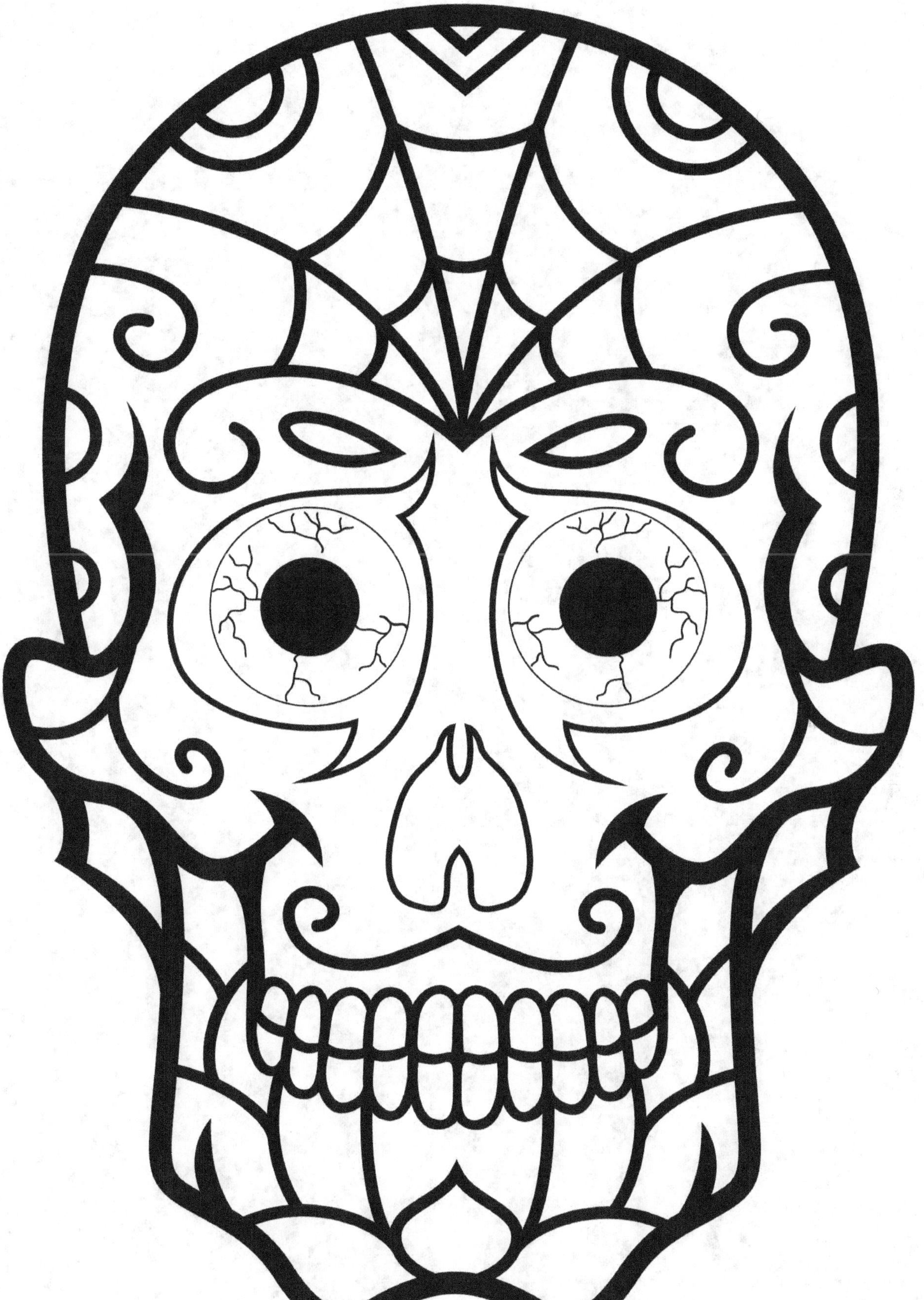

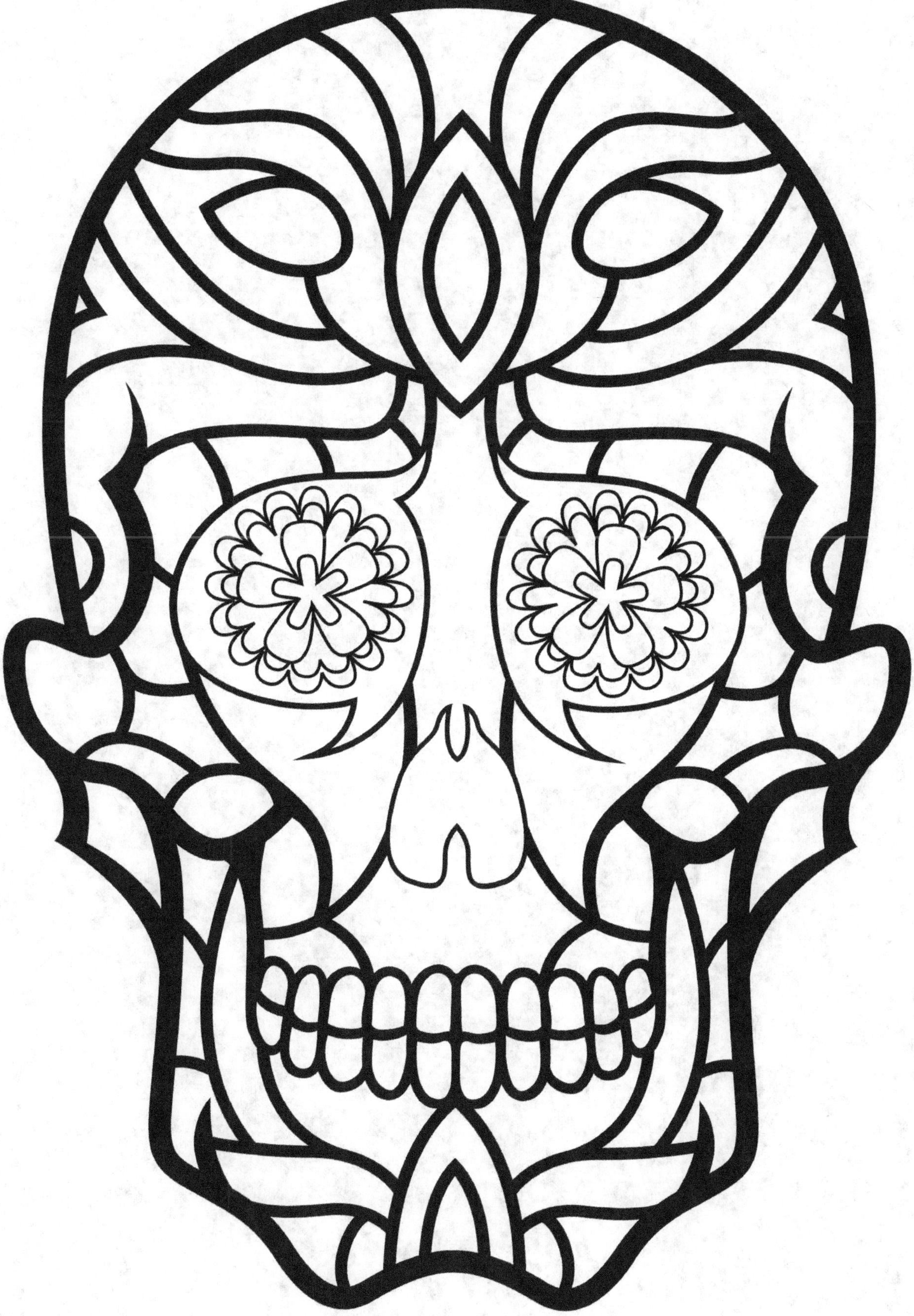

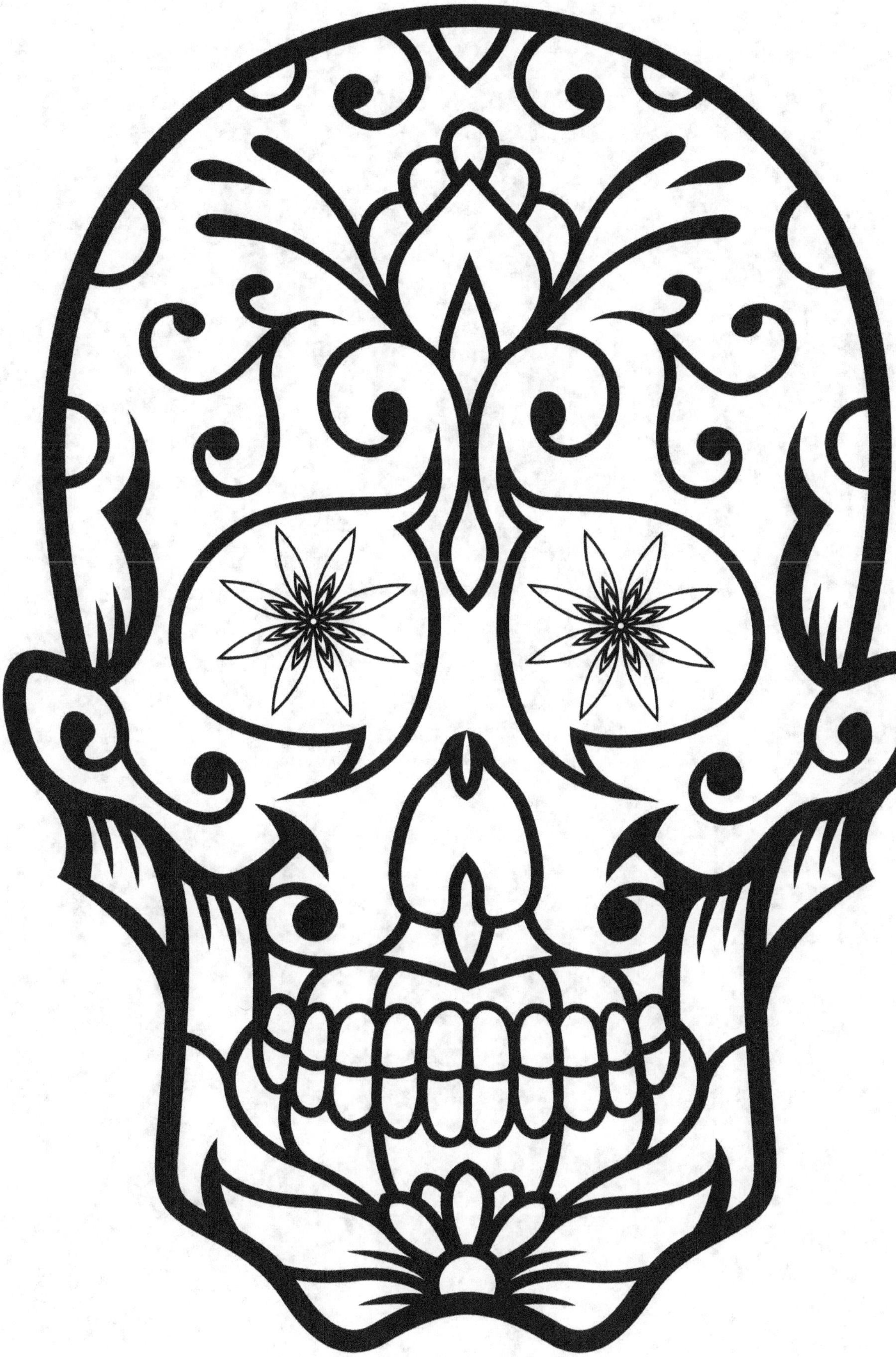

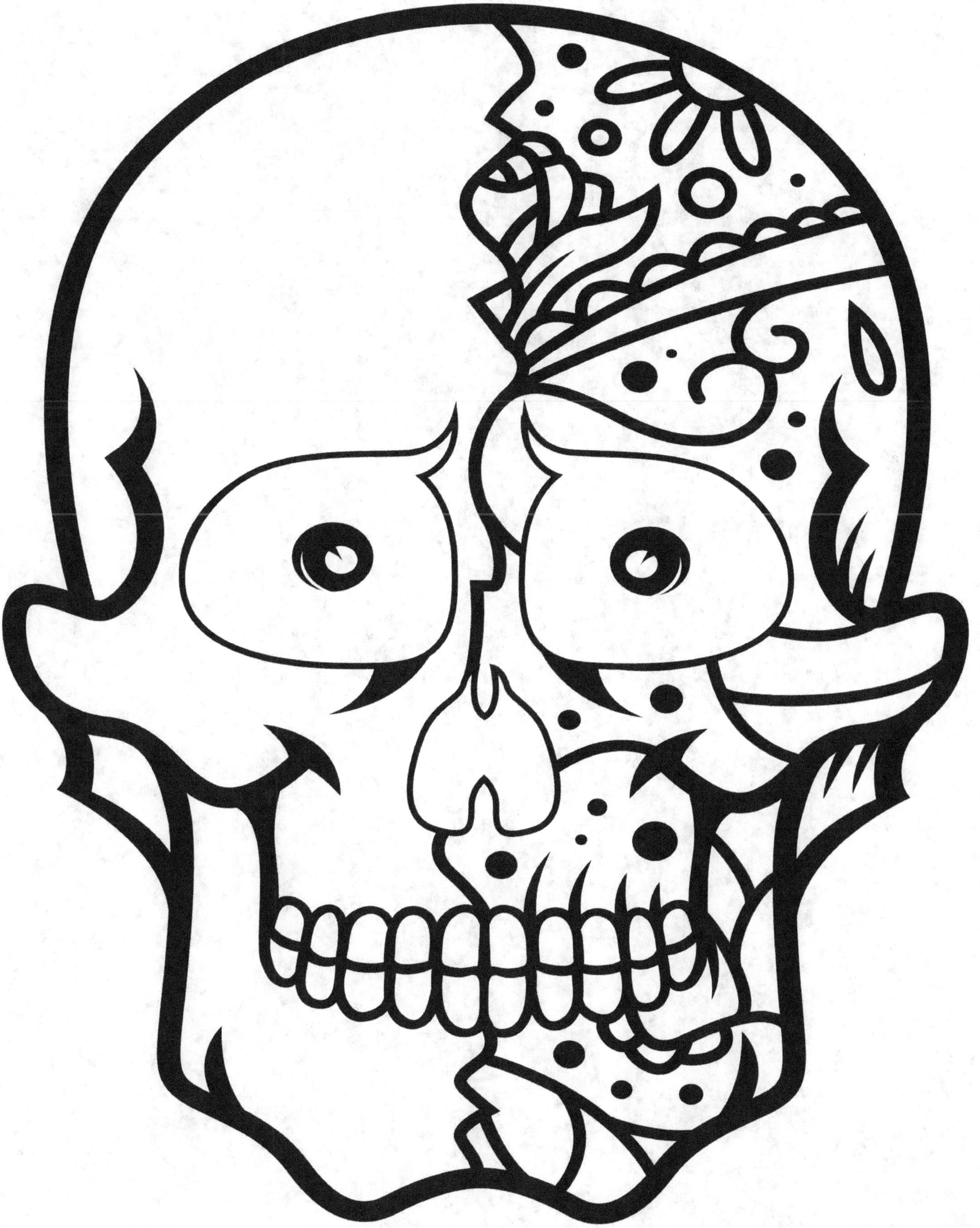

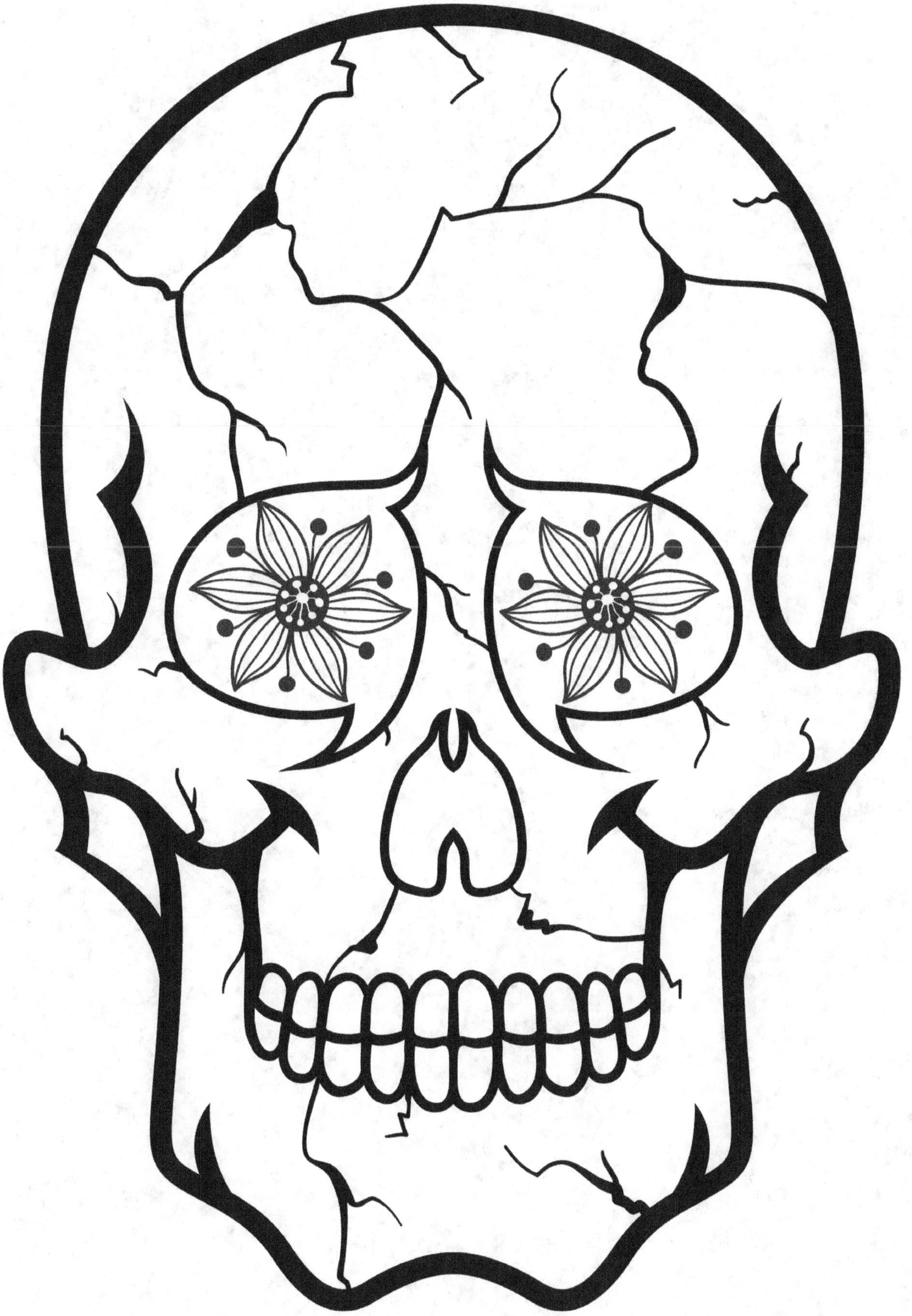

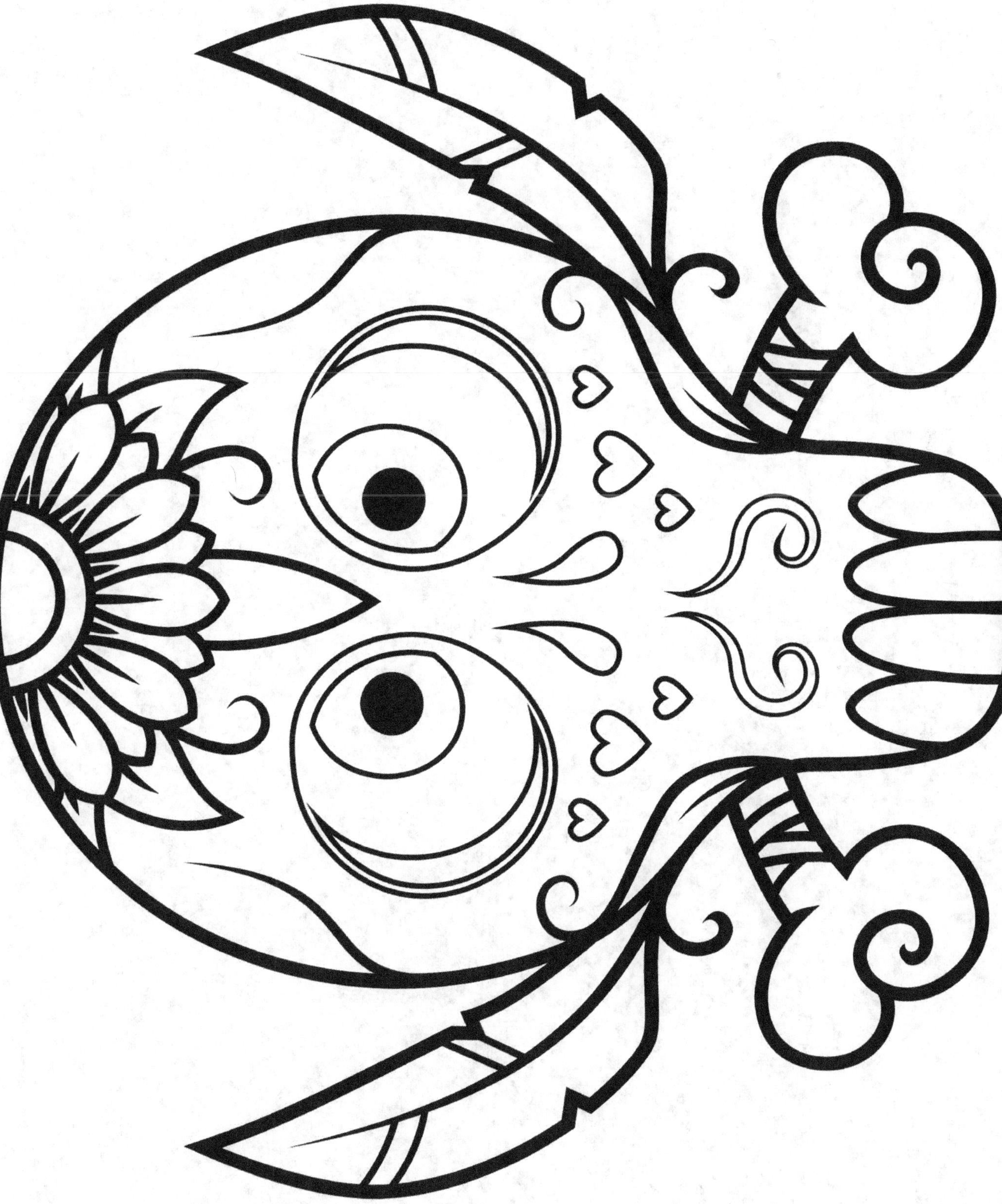

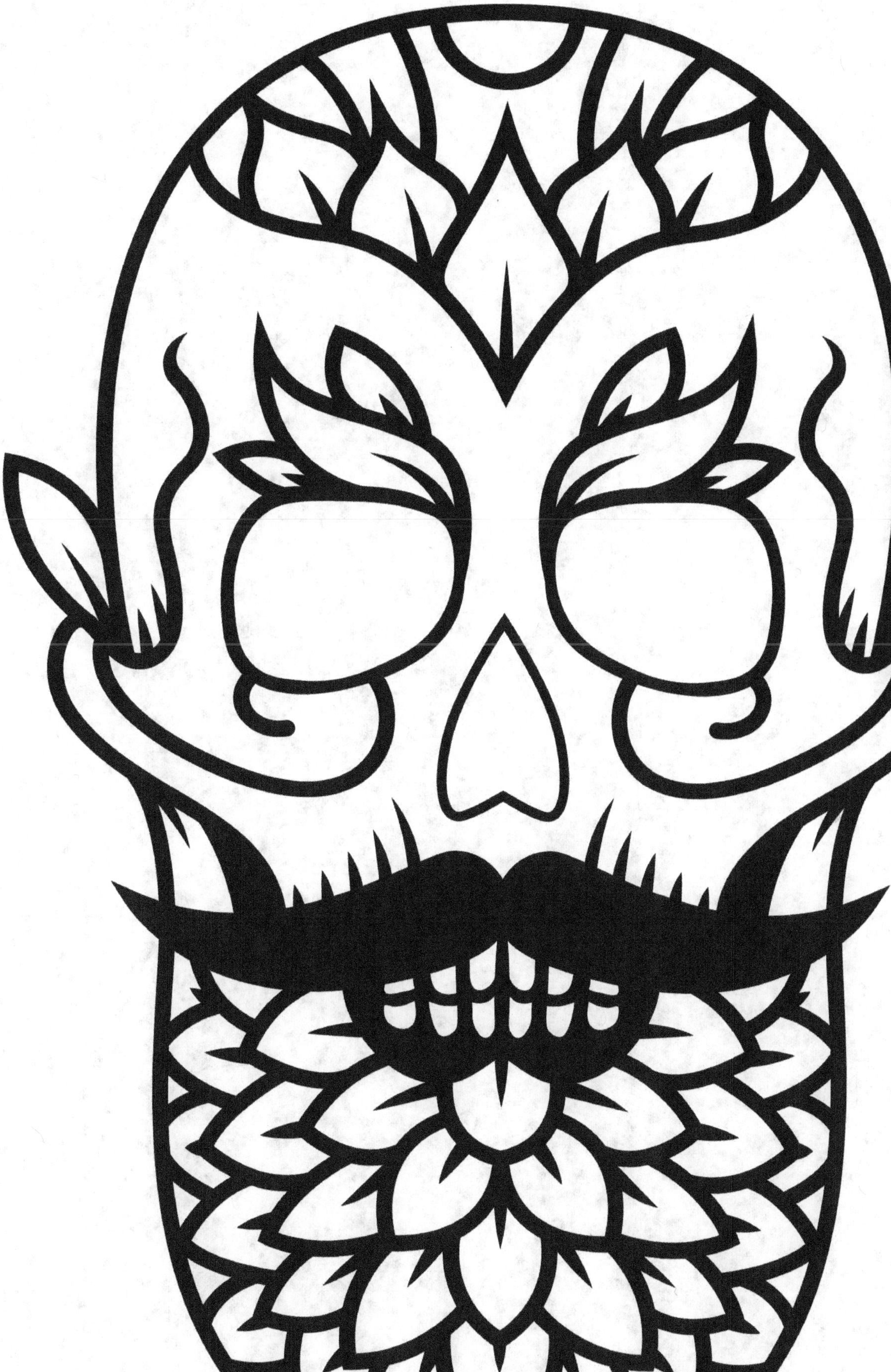

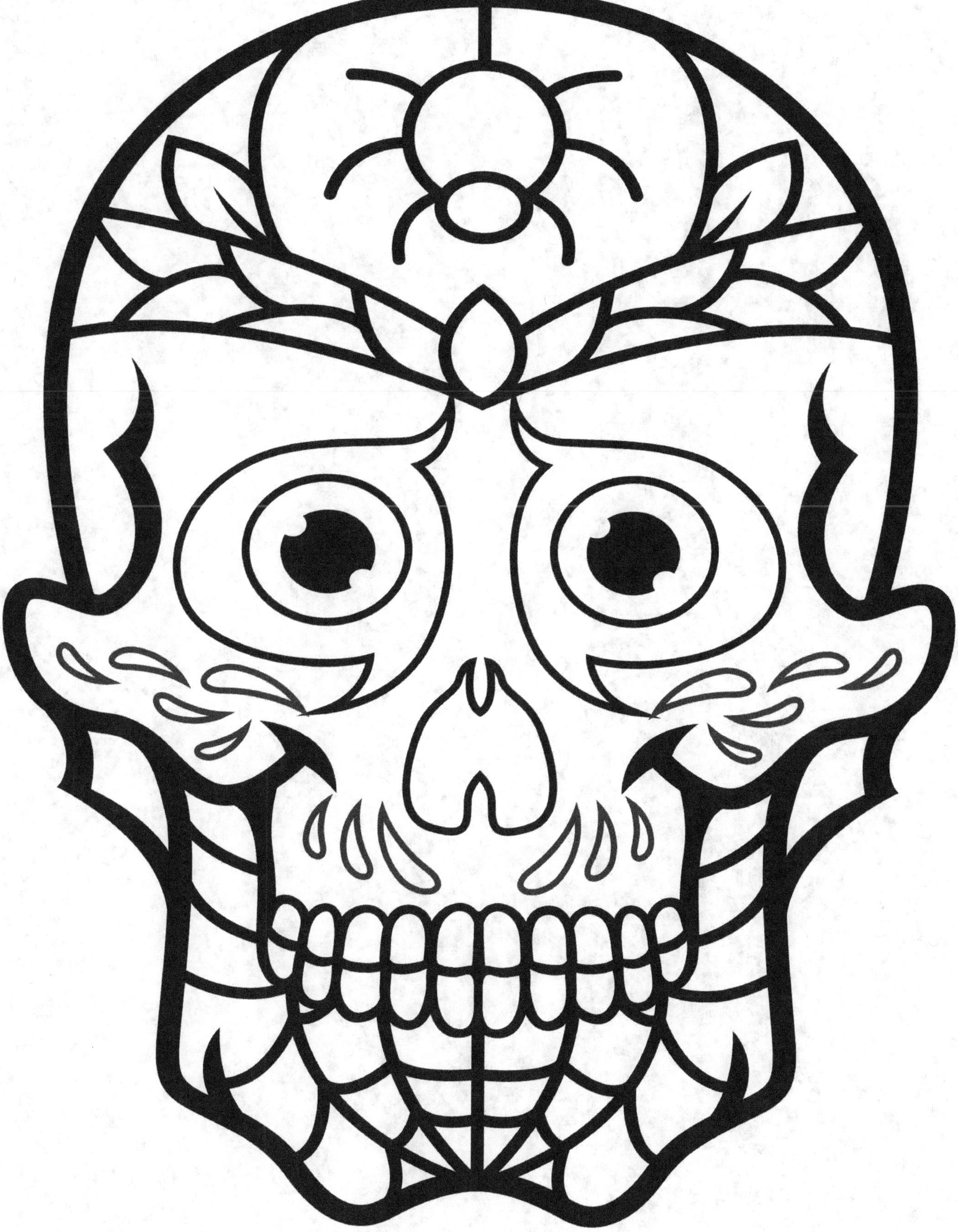

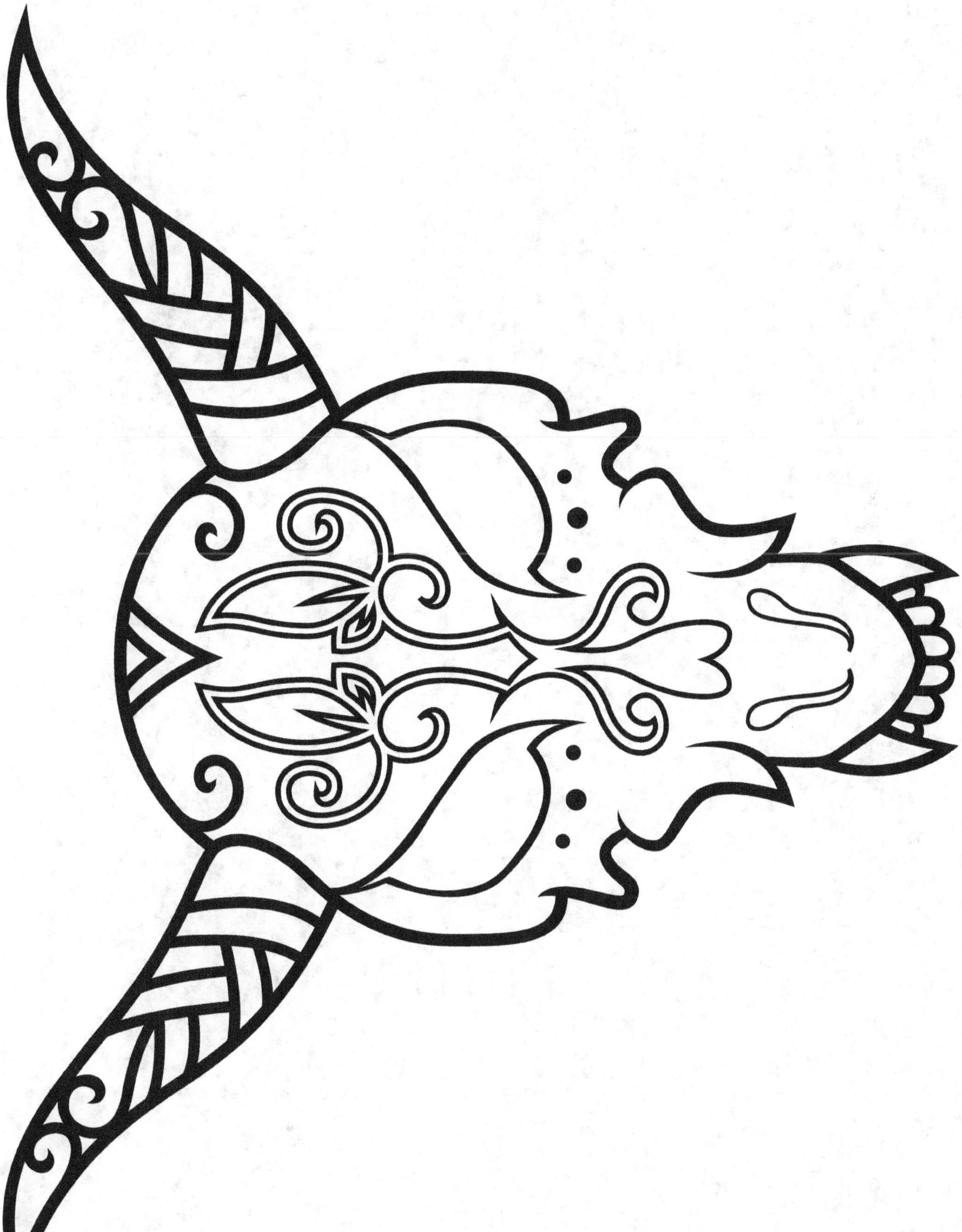

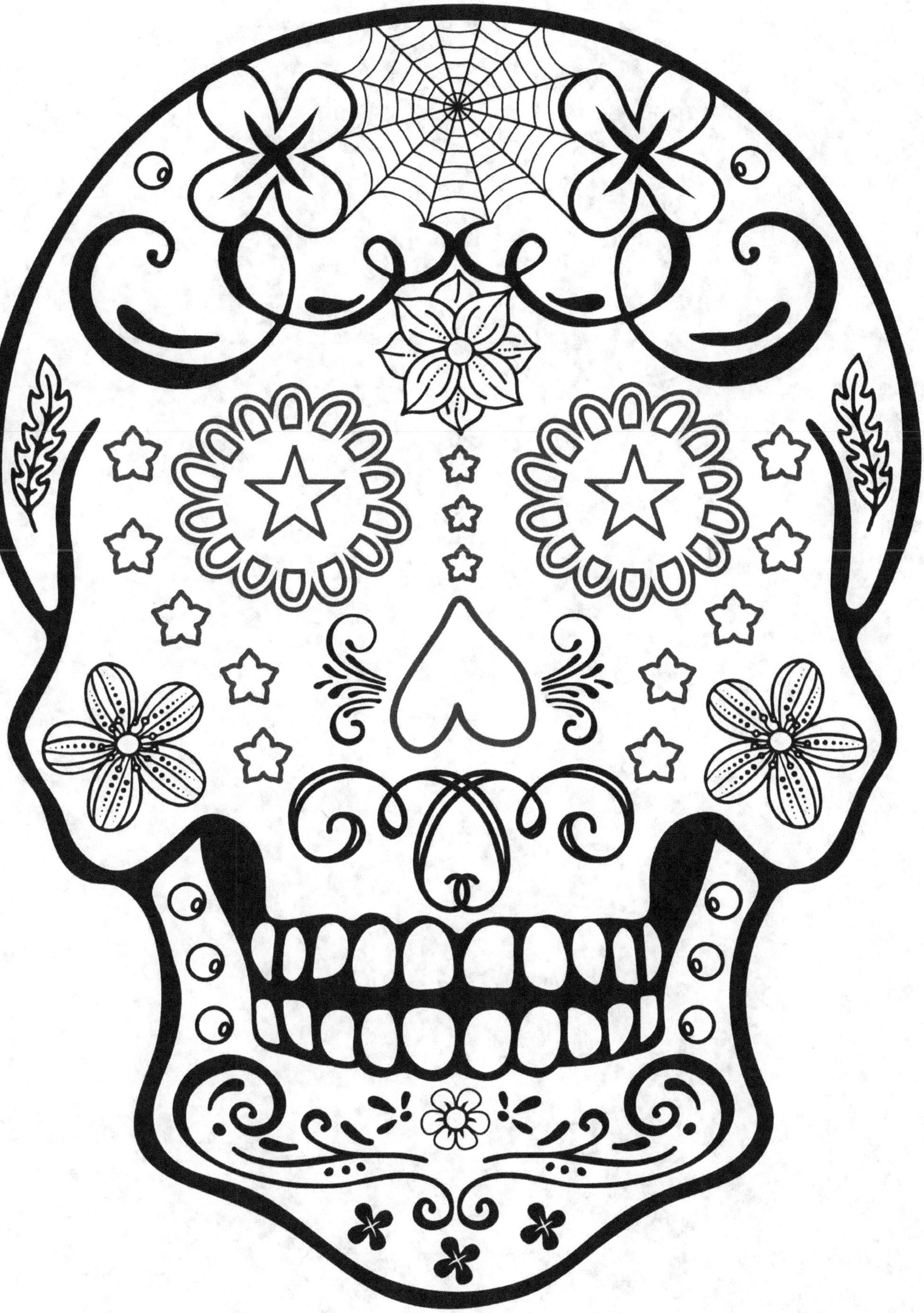

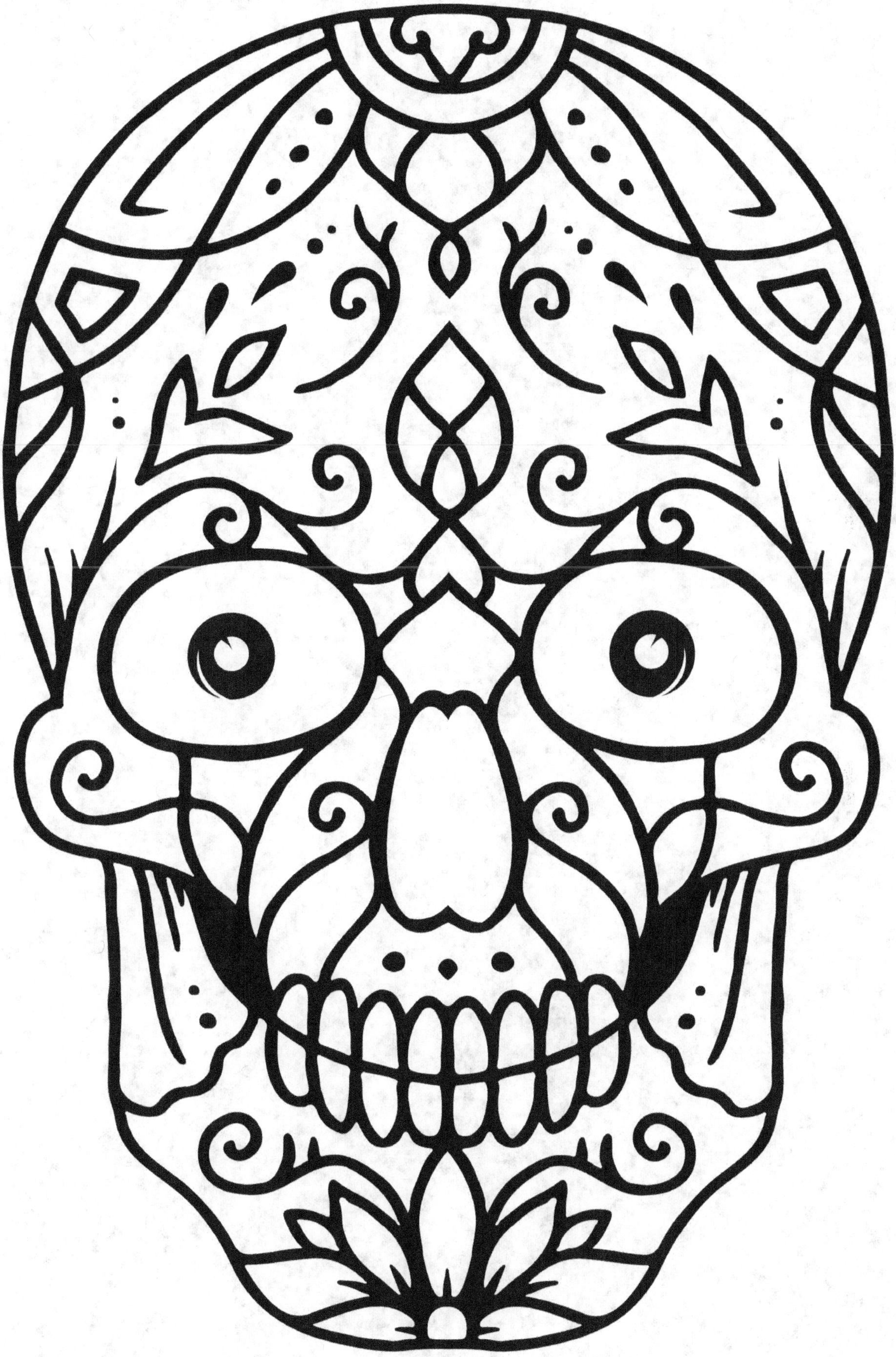

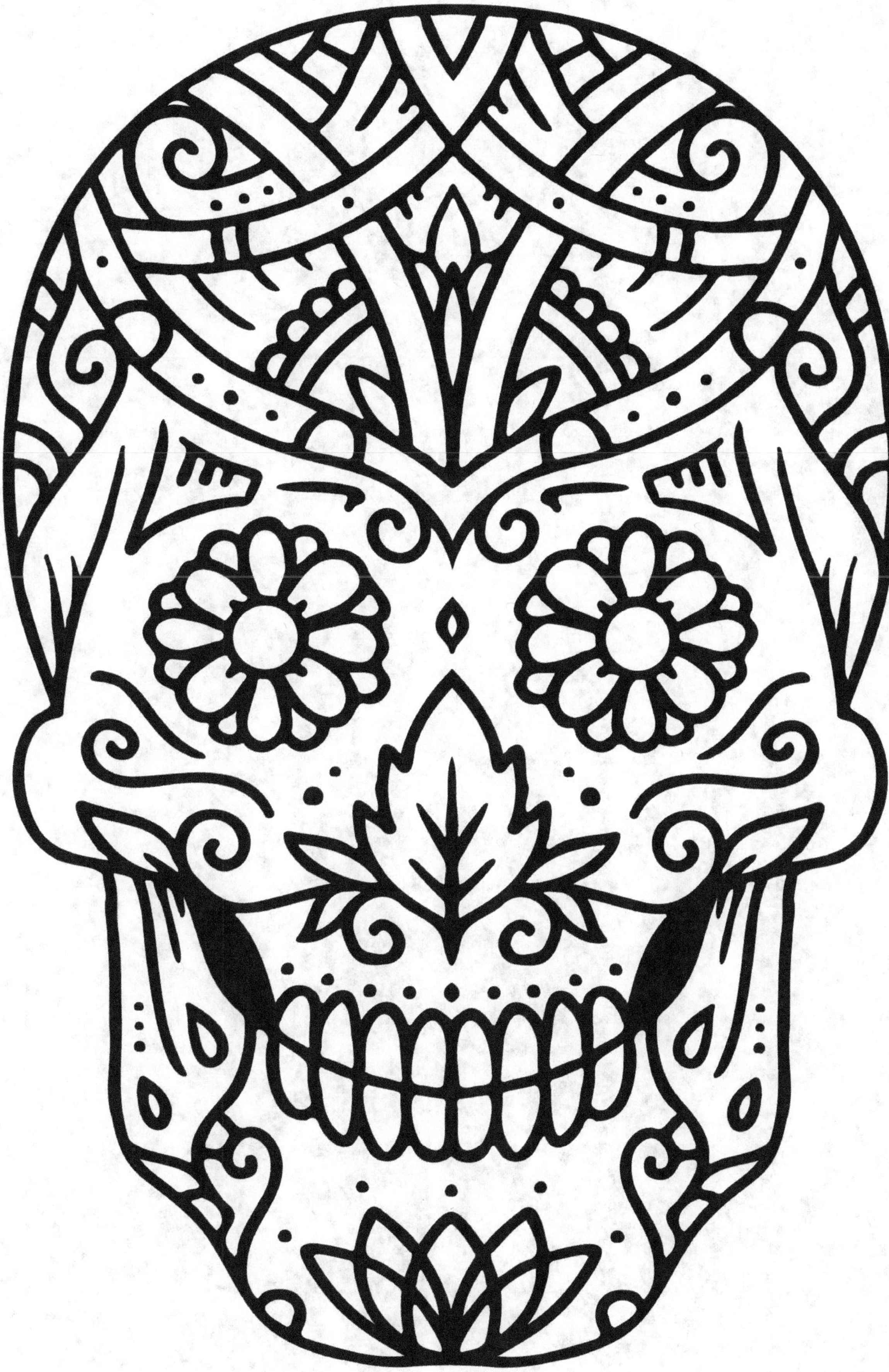

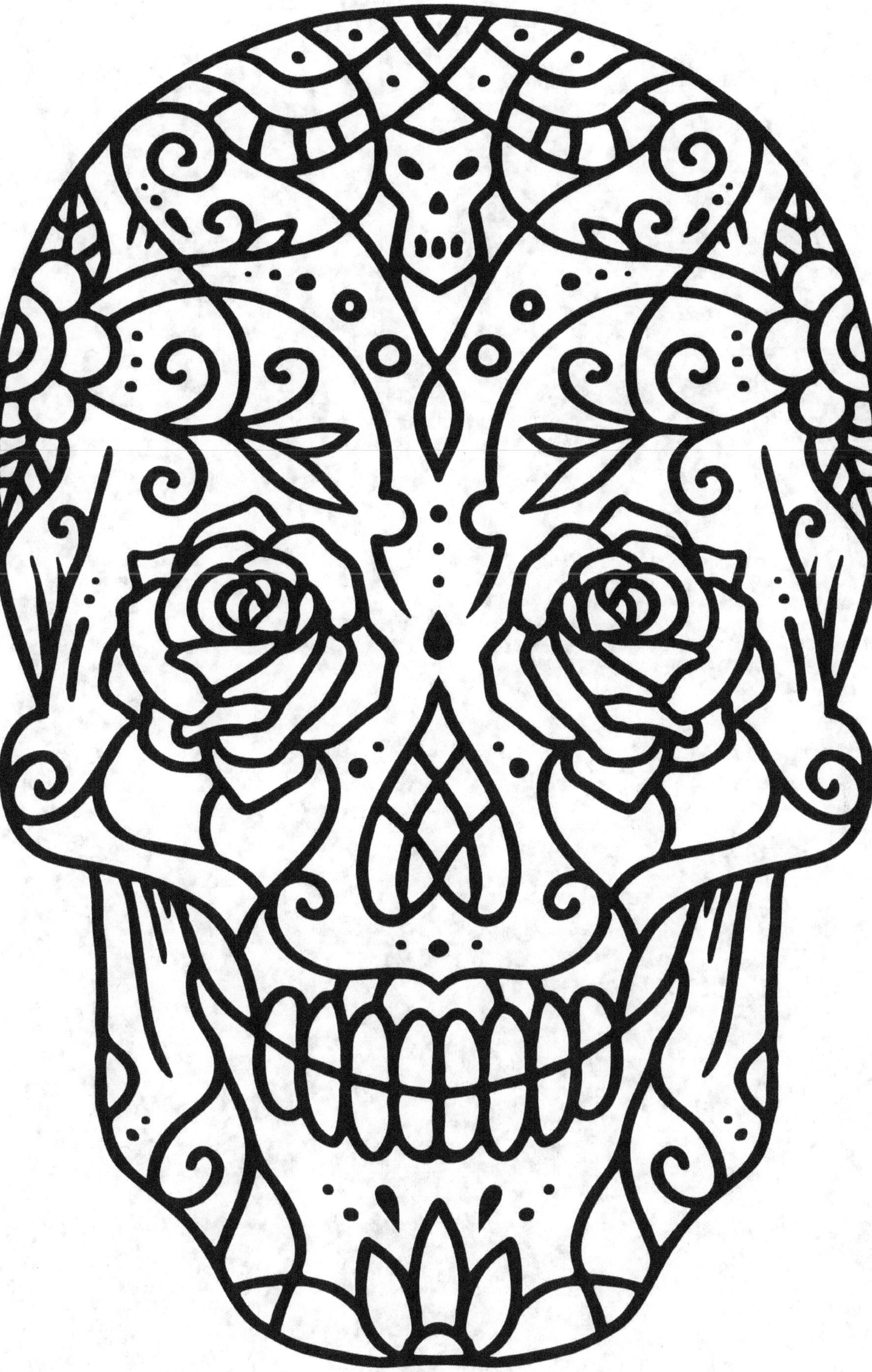

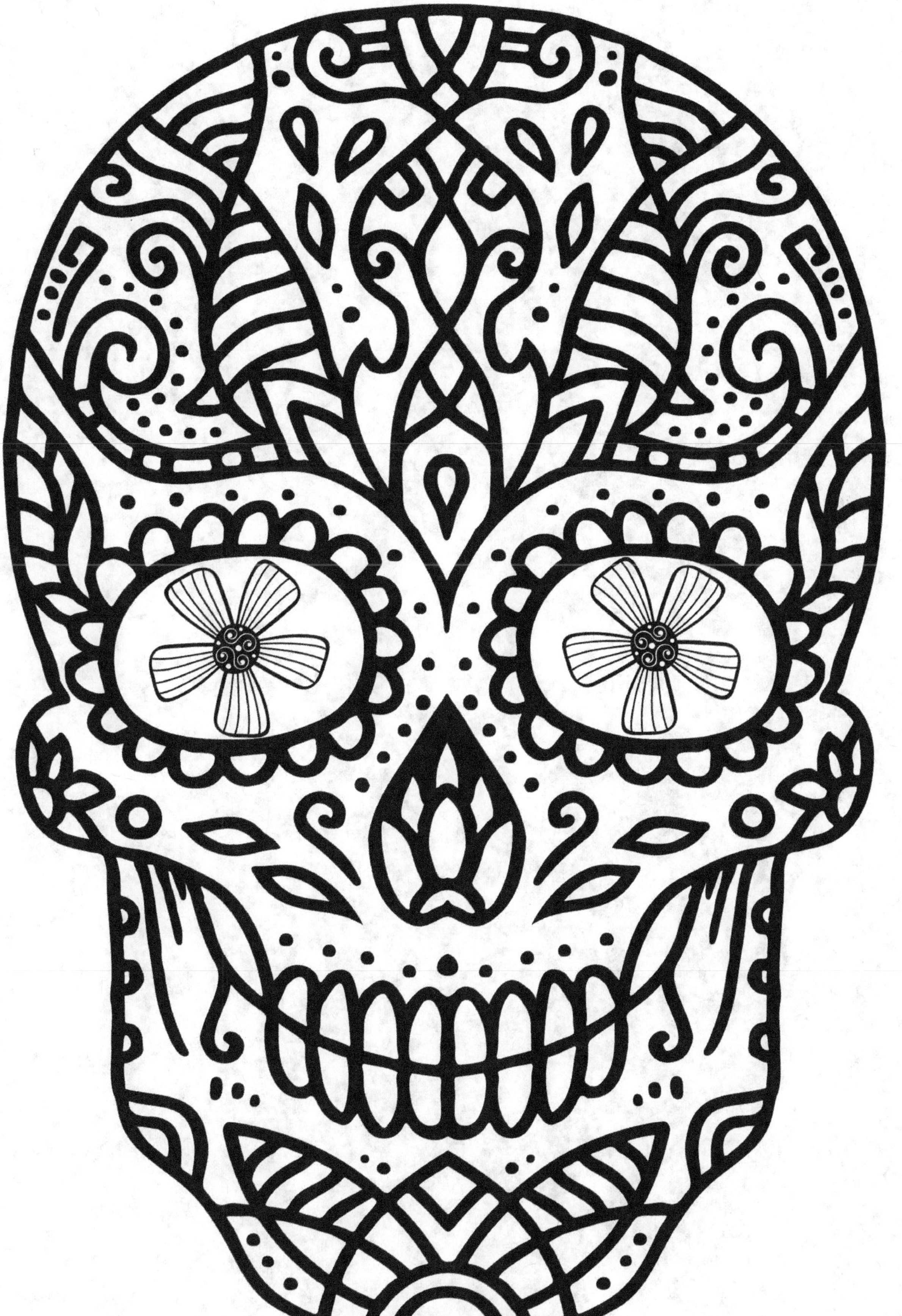

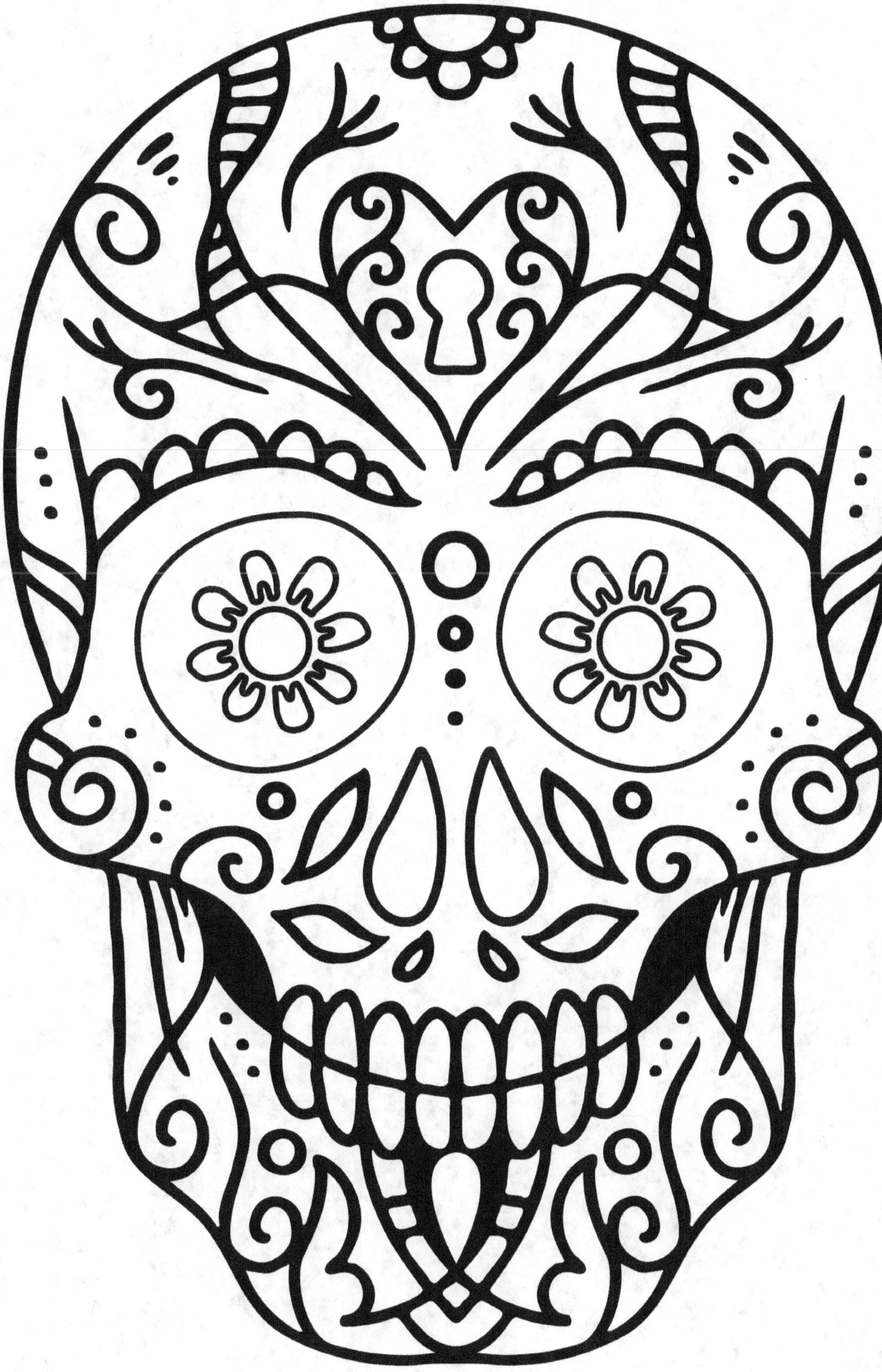

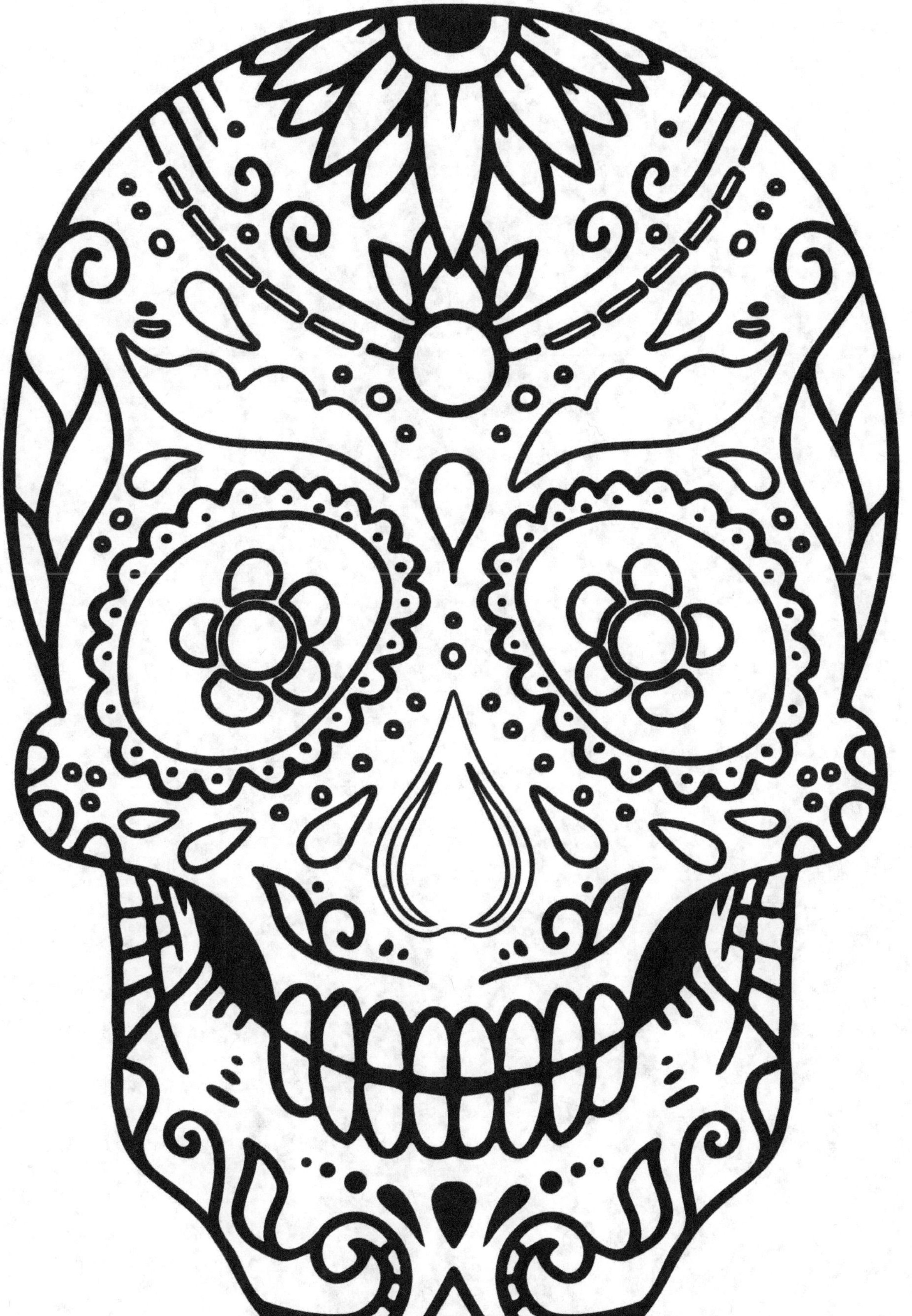

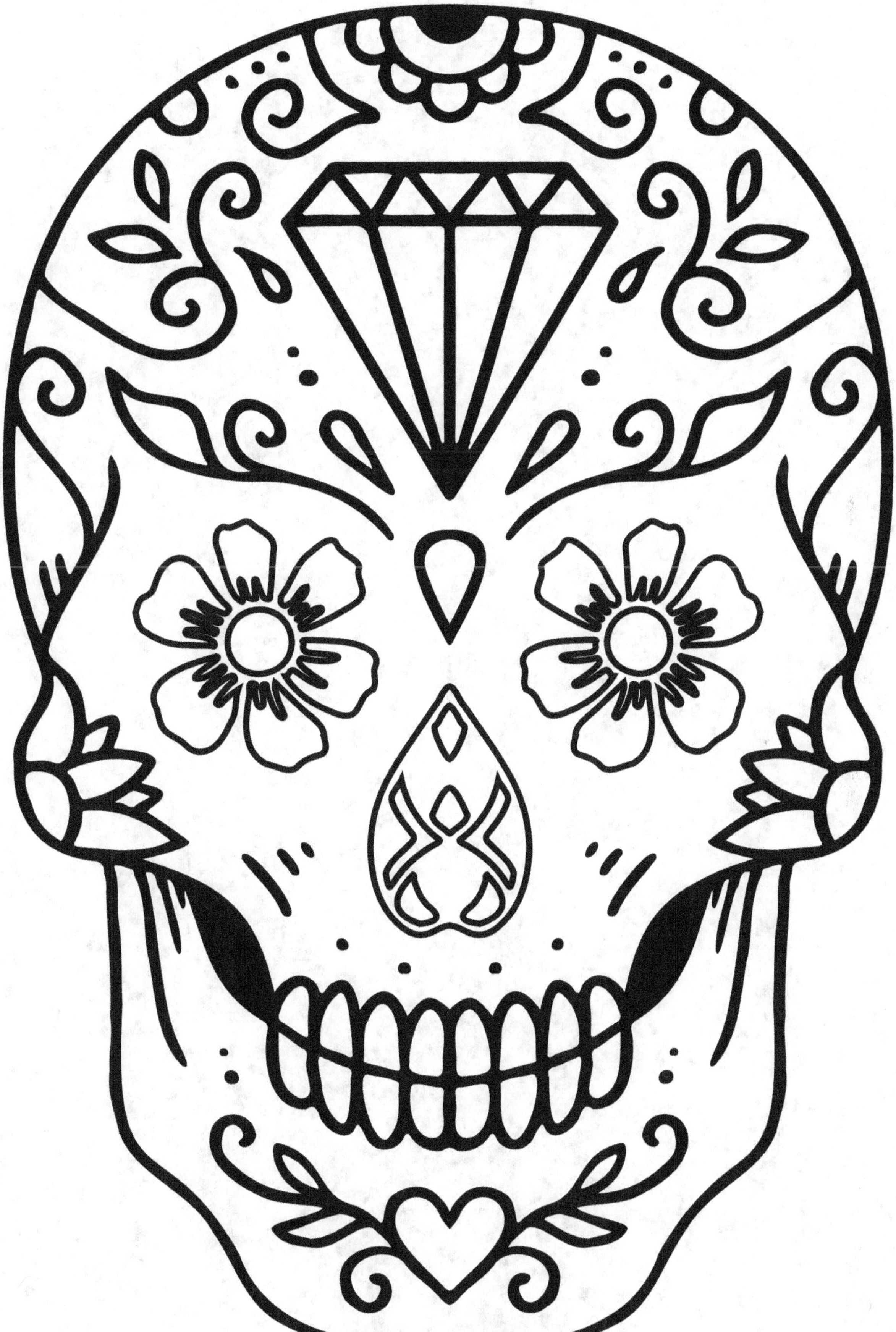

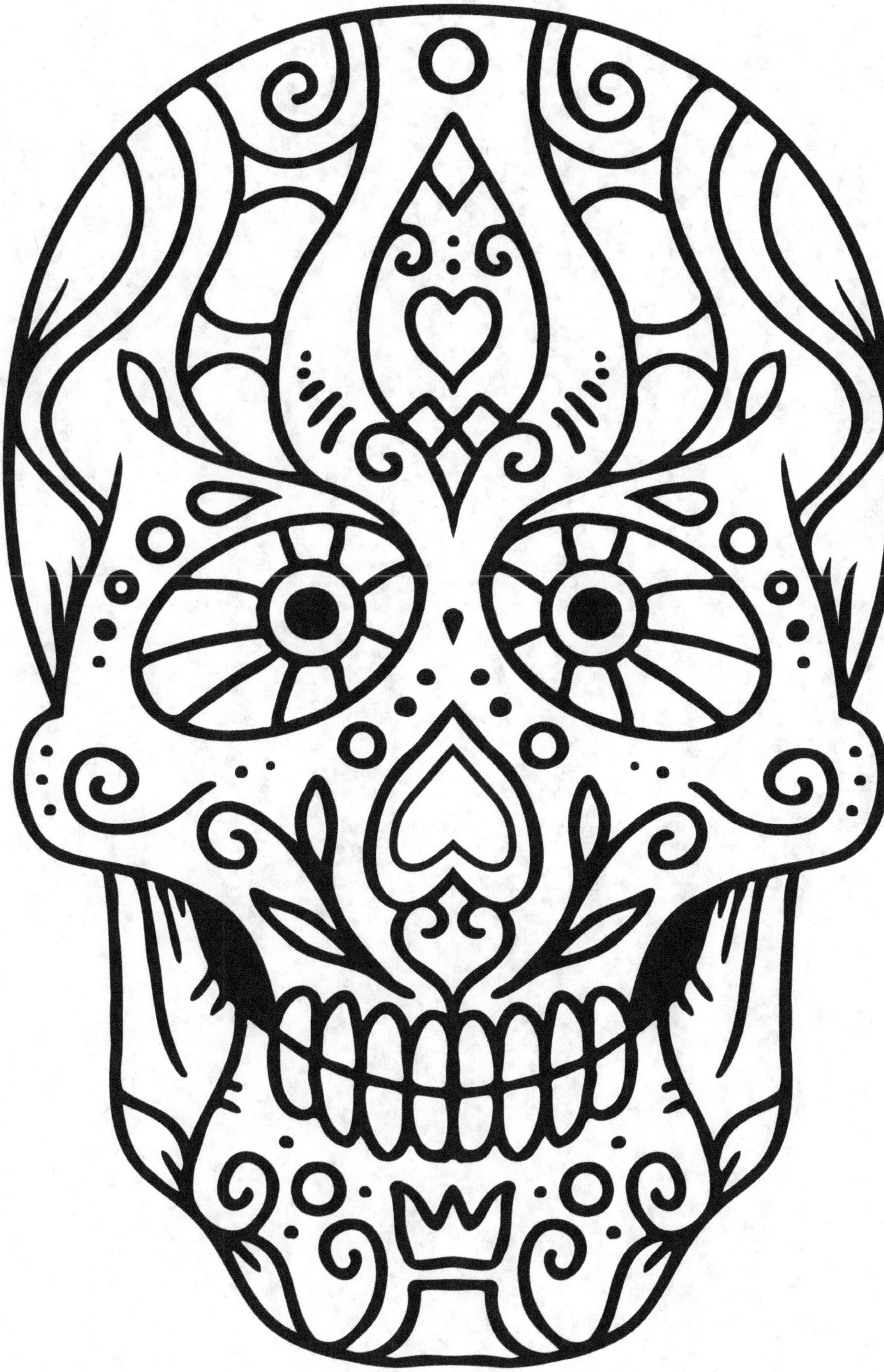

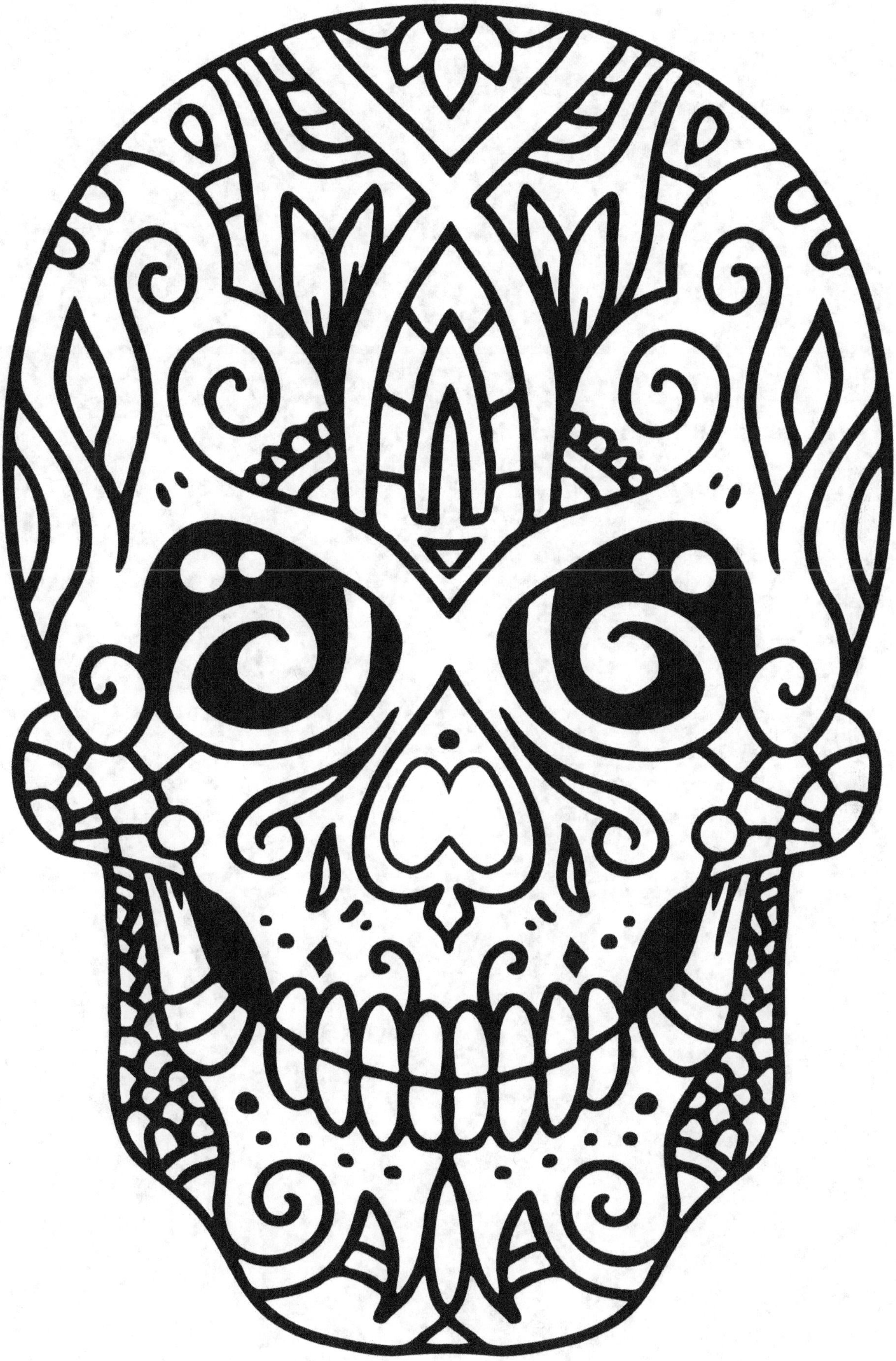

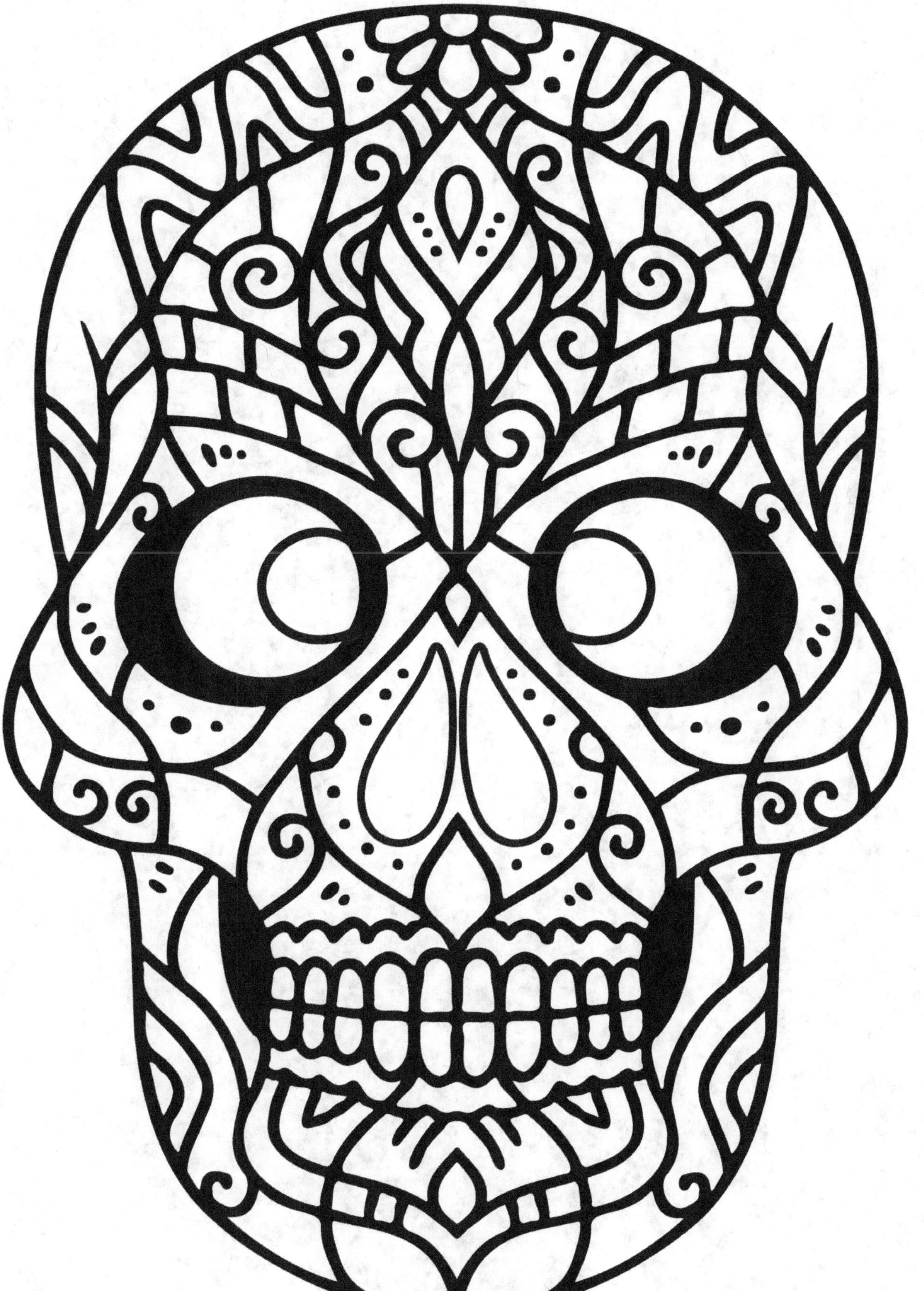

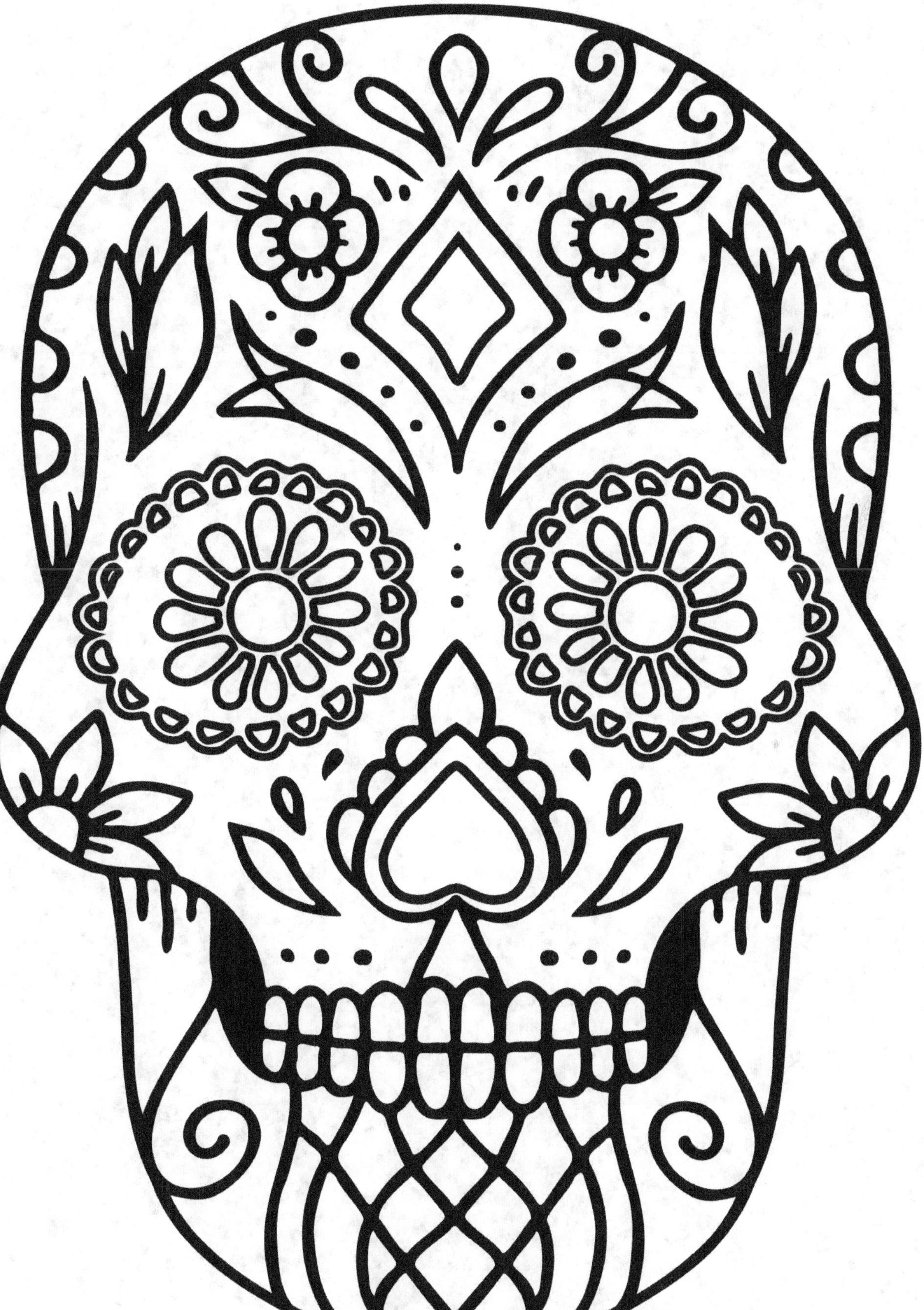

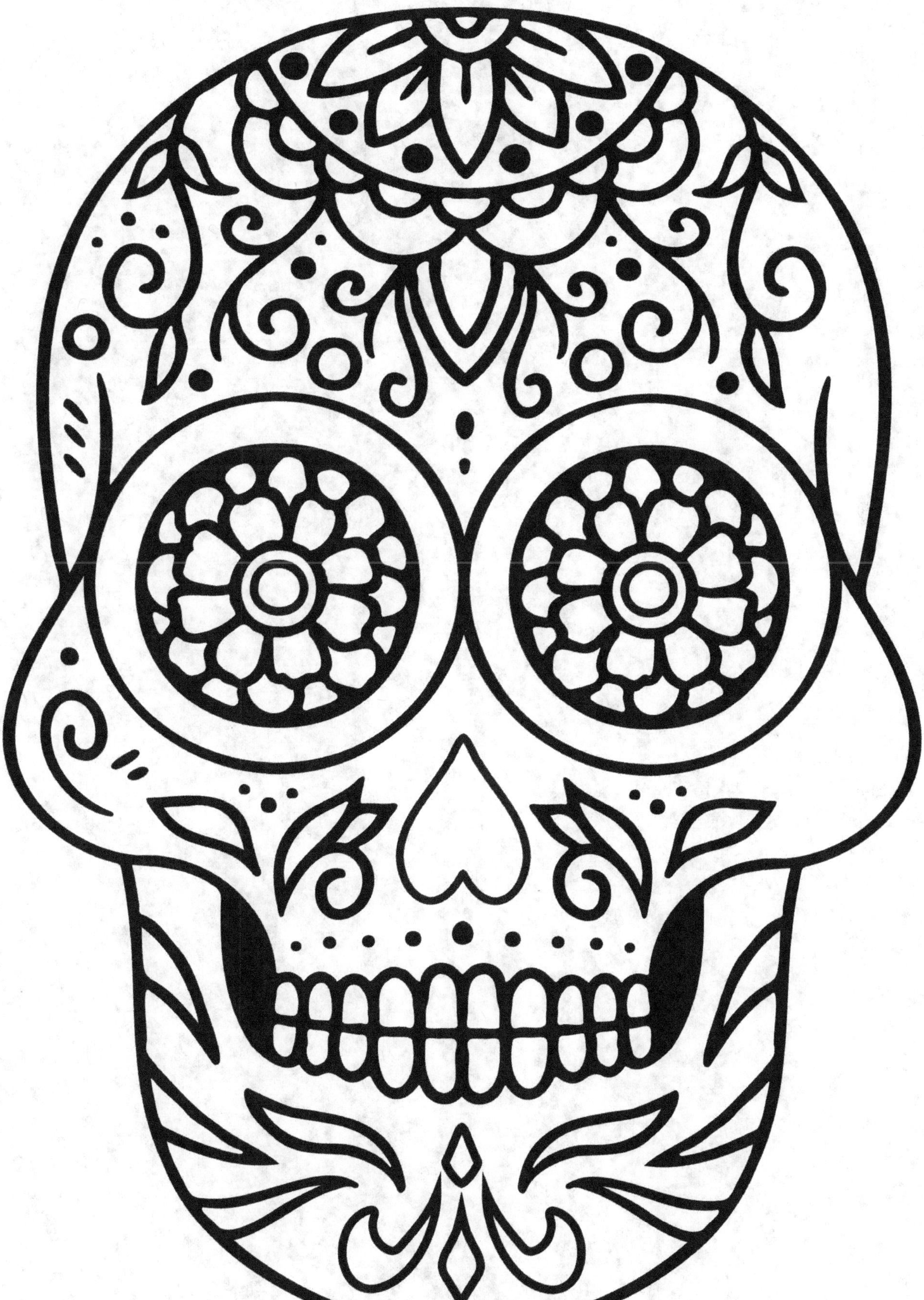

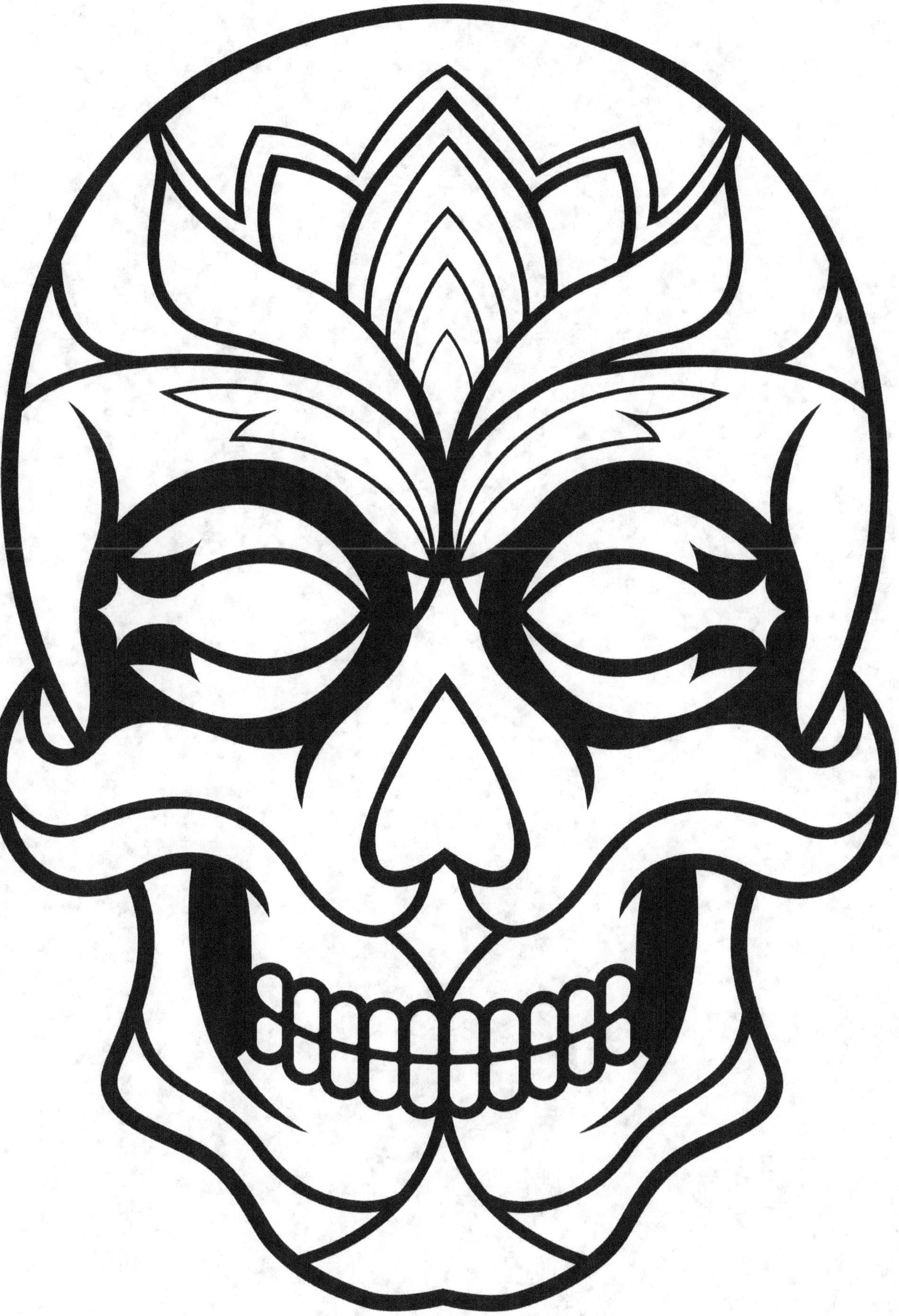

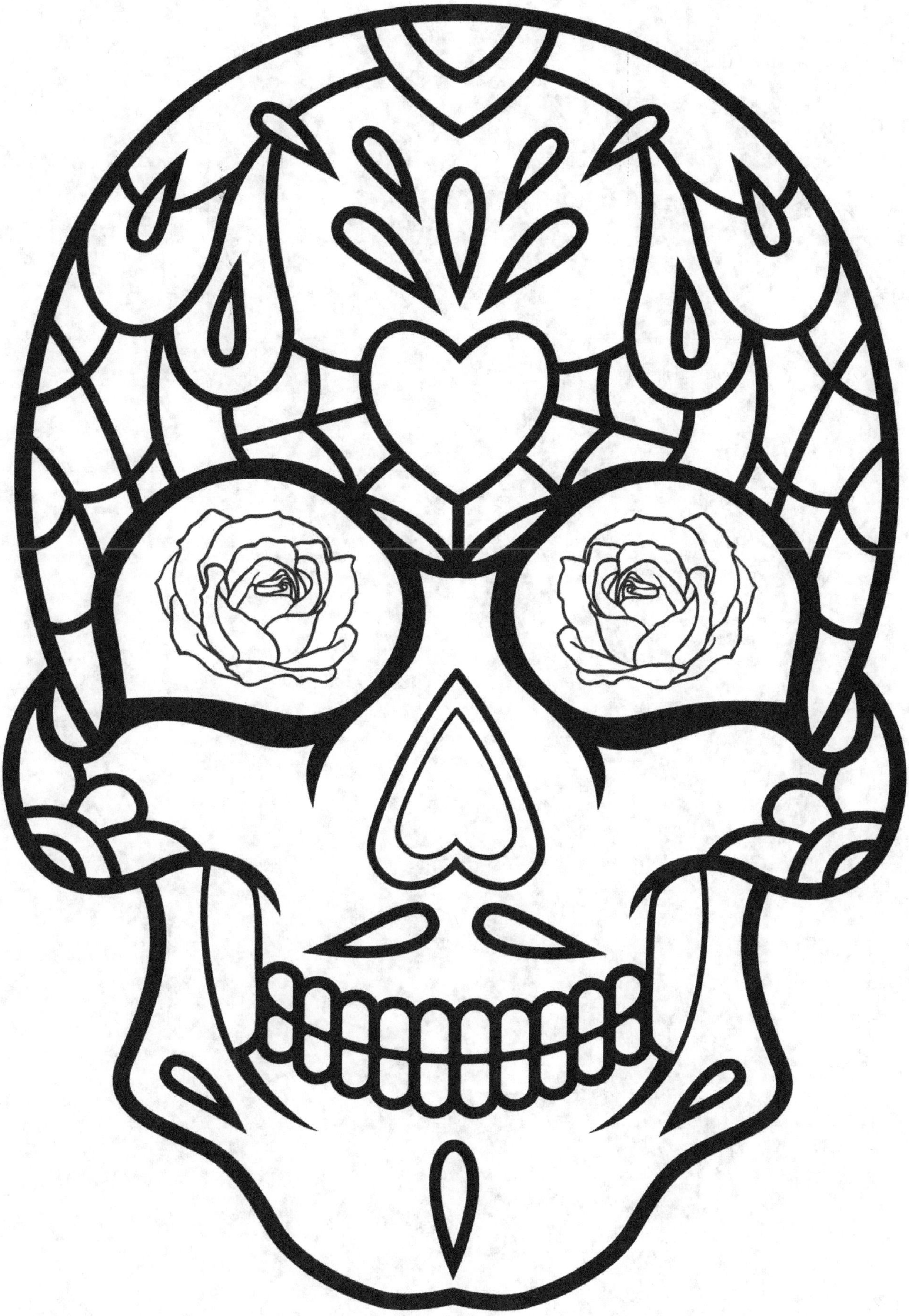

Get your Freebies right now!

Hi there, thanks for purchasing this Sugar Skull coloring book, I guess you enjoyed coloring all those decorated skulls and shared your artworks with your family or friend, if you didn't just do it now!

Please make sure to get in touch with us at this email: Atomipublishing90@gmail.com to receive your free set of sugar skulls and other great decorative coloring pages;

Before you go, don't hesitate to post about your experience with this book, I want to know how people are satisfied with this coloring book, and if there's something you didn't love about it!

Thanks for your precious time! Wish you good luck.

www.ingramcontent.com/pod-product-compliance
Lightning Source LLC
Chambersburg PA
CBHW080106240526
45466CB00023BB/3202
* 9 7 9 8 5 5 3 8 7 2 0 3 8 *